Big Ideas and Revolutionary Activity

Selected Essays, Talks and Articles by Lois Holzman

Edited by
Carrie Lobman and Tony Perone

©2018 East Side Institute
All rights reserved.

Design and layout by Alison Josephs

For information contact:
Melissa Meyer
East Side Institute
119 West 23rd Street, Suite 902
New York, New York 10023
mmeyer@eastsideinstitute.org
(212) 941-8906

"Performing the World: The performance turn in social activism" first appeared in A. Citron, S Aronson-Lehavi and D. Zerbib (Eds.), *Performance studies in motion: International perspectives and practices in the twenty-first century* (2014). It is reprinted with permission from Bloomsbury Publishing.

"Power, authority and pointless activity (The developmental discourse of social therapy)" first appeared in T. Strong and D. Paré (Eds.), *Furthering talk: Advances in the discursive therapies* (2004). It is reprinted with permission from Kluwer Academic/Plenum.

"Without creating ZPDs there is no creativity" first appeared in C. Connery, V. John-Steiner and A. Marjanovic-Shane (Eds.), *Vygotsky and creativity: A cultural-historical approach to play, meaning making, and the arts* (2010). It is reprinted with permission from Peter Lang Publishers.

"The development community and its activist psychology" first appeared in R. House, D. Kalisch and J. Maldman (Eds.), *The future of humanistic psychology* (2013). It is reprinted with permission from Routledge.

"'Vygotskian-izing' psychotherapy" first appeared in *Mind, Culture, and Activity* (2014). It is reprinted with permission from Taylor and Francis.

"All power to the developing!" first appeared in the *Annual Review of Critical Psychology* (2003) and is reprinted with their permission.

"Relating to people as revolutionaries" first appeared in D. Loewenthal, (Ed.), *Critical psychotherapy, psychoanalysis and counselling: Implications for practice* (2015). It is reprinted with permission from Palgrave MacMillan.

— TABLE OF CONTENTS —

A Revolutionary Life 1

Articles and Chapters

    Ludwig Wittgenstein, The Tortured Smarty Pants: 17
    A World Class Thinker Who Taught Us the Dangers of Knowing

    Relating to People as Revolutionaries 25

    "Vygotskian-izing" Psychotherapy 37

    Performing the World: The Performance Turn in Social Activism 55

    Without Creating ZPDs There Is No Creativity 73

    Power, Authority and Pointless Activity 87
    (The Developmental Discourse of Social Therapy)

Invited Talks

    Creating Communities of Hope. 101

    The Diagnostic Debate: Voices from the Street 113

    Social Therapy and Creating an Activist Life 125

    Vygotsky on the Margins: A Global Search for Method 133

Blog Posts

    Activist-Scholars: A Story Within a Story 143

    Play as if Your Mental Health Depended on It 151

    'We're Not Buying It!" — Survey on Emotional Distress 155
    and Diagnosis Reveals Mistrust of Psychiatric Labeling

    Holiday Warning: Giving Can Change Your Life!. 157

    Why Ask Why? Sometimes We Just Need to Move On. 161

    Danger! A Frightening New Mental Illness 163

    The Surprising Secret of Why Therapy Works 165

    A New Way of Seeing Development (Hint: We Make It Happen) 167

    The Biggest Myths About Emotions & How to Weaken Their Grip 169

    Performing—A New Way to Live 171

    A Diagnosis the DSM-5 Forgot—Physics Envy. 173

    Developmental Play for All. 175

    Become a Vygotskian!. 177

    Why Knowing Keeps Us Dumb 179

Meet the Editors 181

Acknowledgements

The editors would like to thank Mary Fridley,
Dan Friedman, Margo Grant, Alison Josephs, Jordan Timmers,
Rachael A. Williamson and Jan Wootten for their
invaluable help and support with this project.
We could not have done it without you!

— A REVOLUTIONARY LIFE —

LOIS HOLZMAN is an international activist who has combined rigorous scholarship with grassroots community organizing. She is a leader of an ongoing community building activity involving thousands of people around the world who are engaging the material and conceptual restraints on human development and progressive social change. Lois' life-as-lived challenges the theory/practice divide. She is equally at home talking postmodernism with a group of teenagers from a poor community like East New York, Brooklyn, as she is engaging in improv games with faculty and students at the Tsukuba University in Tokyo. Whether this is your first time "meeting" Lois or you have followed her for years, we offer you this introduction as a way to learn more about her revolutionary life and as an entrée to the articles, chapters, talks and blog posts that make up this volume.

Lois has always gone beyond the boundaries of mainstream scholarship. Her doctoral dissertation challenged the prevailing understandings of language development, and her post-doctoral work at the Laboratory of Comparative Human Development at Rockefeller University confronted the legitimacy of the laboratory as a means of studying human beings. The most radical decision of Lois' career came in 1976 when she met Dr. Fred Newman and joined him and a nascent group of community activists who were working to translate "the most progressive ideals of the 1960s into effective instruments of social and personal transformation" (http://frednewman-phd.com/about-fred-newman).

Newman, who passed away in 2011, had received his PhD in analytic philosophy and foundations of mathematics from Stanford University in 1962 and had gone on to teach philosophy at several colleges and universities. In 1969, at the height of the social movements of that decade, he left academia to pursue community and political organizing. His reasons were both political and ethical. In the face of the failure of the Great Society programs, Newman and his colleagues wanted to create—from the bottom up in partnership with the community--new institutions for addressing poverty and its devastating impact. Over the next four decades Newman was the catalyst and chief architect for building sustained, community-based developmental psychological, educational, electoral and cultural projects independently funded and volunteer driven. While his academic training was in philosophy, Newman went on to become a group psychotherapist, an award-winning playwright and the political strategist and campaign manager for Dr. Lenora Fulani's historic runs for President of the United States in 1988 and 1992.

After meeting Newman in the late 1970s Lois became his chief intellectual collaborator and a leader of what has grown into the international "development community." In the 1980s Newman and Lois co-founded the East Side Institute for Group and Short Term Psychotherapy which has served as the home for their independent scholarship and innovative practices. The practices that emerged from their partnership reflected

Big Ideas and Revolutionary Activity

a synthesis of their intellectual training and the learning that comes from a day-to-day community-building practice. Lois worked with Newman on the development of a social therapeutic methodology, an approach that Newman had begun as one of many radical alternatives to traditional psychotherapy in the 1960s. Social therapeutics has transformed into a postmodern, sociocultural methodology for reinitiating human development--in the therapy room and on the streets. The approach is now practiced around the world in outside-of-school programs for young people, formal and informal educational settings for children and adults, medicine and healthcare—including in dementia care—and organizational development and executive leadership, and it informs an increasing number of community organizing initiatives around the world.

The "Newman/Holzman" collaboration produced many books, articles and presentations including *Lev Vygotsky: Revolutionary Scientist* (Newman & Holzman, 1993), *Unscientific Psychology: A Cultural Performatory Approach to Understanding Human Life* (Newman & Holzman, 1996), and *The End of Knowing: A New Developmental Way of Learning* (Newman & Holzman, 2006). The current volume consists primarily of Lois' work since Newman's death in 2011, and the remainder of this introduction focuses on her. However, it is important to acknowledge that the longevity and impact of their collaboration makes such a separation artificial, and we consider this book a tribute to their partnership and to the community that sustained and was enriched by it.

So, it is clear that in leaving the academy Lois did not leave intellectual work behind. Far from it. A quick scan of this volume suggests that freeing herself from the constraints of the university and partnering with Newman allowed Lois to develop as a scholar and to make discoveries about human development, learning, language, diagnosis, play and performance that would have been impossible from within traditional disciplinary silos and university expectations. Lois is well known for her pioneering work in exploring the human capacity to perform and its essential role in learning how to learn. She is a leader of the growing international play and performance movement that is touching the lives of thousands around the United States and globally.

She has, in both theory and practice, successfully demonstrated that Vygotsky's (1978, p. 102) discovery that in play children perform "a head taller" than they are, is also true of older children and adults, and that play and performance are too valuable to be left only to little children and professional actors. As the founder and chief organizer of the biennial Performing the World conferences, Lois leads an international community that takes a performance approach in addressing educational, mental health, and health and social policy issues. In addition, she has initiated collaborative cultural/psychological/community-building projects among psychologists, social workers and educators from the United States and a growing list of other countries, including Argentina, Bangladesh, Brazil, Canada, China, Colombia, Denmark, India, Japan, Mexico, Peru, Serbia, South Africa, Taiwan, Uganda and the United Kingdom.

Selected Essays, Talks and Articles by Lois Holzman

Lois has written, co-written, or edited 10 books and over 70 articles and chapters. on human development and learning, psychology, education and social therapy including: *Vygotsky at Work and Play* (2017) and her latest book, *The Overweight Brain: How our Obsession with Knowing Keeps Us from Getting Smart Enough to Make a Better World* (2018) which she wrote online with active participation from her audience. The current volume, *Big Ideas and Revolutionary Activity*, brings together a curated selection of Lois' (mostly recent) writings. This is not meant to be a comprehensive anthology; our objective is to provide people with a taste of the range of Lois' work in terms of subject matter, style and audience. We hope it will inspire you to read more of her work, make use of it in your own teaching, learning, community organizing, scholarship and any other revolutionary activities you are part of, and in doing so, delve deeper into it.

Meet the Editors
So, who is this "we" that we speak of? We are Carrie Lobman and Tony Perone, and we are university professors in the fields of education and psychology, respectively. Of course, this is not all of who we are. We are also community organizers, performance activists, play revolutionaries, comedic improvisers, colleagues and dear friends. We each had the fortune of meeting Lois early in our careers and, over the years, she has been our mentor and now also our friend and colleague. Throughout this introduction we have chosen to refer to Lois by her first name and ourselves in the first-person plural; however, when we are giving examples from our own practice we will make sure to identify who is speaking.

We decided to edit this volume because we recognize the value that Lois' writing has brought to our own lives, and we wanted to make it accessible to many more people. As we are both university professors, some of the examples we provide are of how we have utilized Lois' writing in our classroom teaching. However, we also bring in our own work as activists, and we have spoken with other people who bring Lois into a wide range of activities such as therapy, community organizing, youth development, medicine and organizational development. One of the characteristics that everyone expressed is that Lois' writing is rigorous and playful, and so we invite you to delve into the content of this introduction and the selections that follow in that spirit.

Beyond Definitions and Labels
Lois can be described in many ways and in the sections that follow we introduce to you to some of them. Lois herself says, "I don't like labels and so one of the things I play around with is what to call myself." We now share some ways we (and Lois) might play with referring to her(self).

A Methodologist
> The search for method becomes one of the most important problems of the entire enterprise of understanding the uniquely human forms of psychological activity. In this case, the method is simultaneously prerequisite and product, the tool and the result of the study. (Vygotsky, 1978, p. 65)

Big Ideas and Revolutionary Activity

Lois' life-as-lived has been an instantiation of Vygotsky's search for method. From her earliest days as a graduate student Lois has pushed the envelope against the inherent biases and distortions of the research methods and tools used in the social sciences. This challenge intensified when she began working with Fred Newman and participated in the creation of social therapeutics. Starting in the early 1990s they began writing books and articles that challenged the application of the methods of the natural sciences to the social sciences in general, and to psychology in particular. Their seminal book, *Unscientific Psychology: A Cultural Performatory Approach to Understanding Human Life* (1996) deconstructs the history of psychology. It explores how the methods of the natural sciences, which have benefited humanity immensely in the form of advances in physics, chemistry and medicine, have been distortive and destructive when applied to the social/cultural life of human beings. Human beings, they argue, as simultaneously the studier and the studied, cannot use the same tools to research ourselves that are used to study the stars. "People do not merely respond to stimuli, acquire societally determined and useful skills and adapt to the determining environment. The uniqueness of human social life is that we ourselves transform the determining circumstances" (Newman & Holzman, 1993, p. x).

Throughout her career, Lois has given expression to her outrage at the ways in which the pseudo-science of psychology has distorted who we are as human beings and created what she calls a diagnostic way of life. Together with Newman she has written extensively about the ways in which psychology has produced an obsession with explaining and defining who we are at the expense of seeing and continuously creating who we are becoming. Moreover, Lois has not stopped at being a critic of psychology and the other social sciences. Following Karl Marx's understanding of practical-critical, revolutionary activity she has worked to bring into existence new activities, organizations and practices that are in their very existence a challenge to the existing institution of psychology. These have included a therapy practice where clients are helped with their emotional problems without the use of diagnosis or explanation, an experimental independent school where children and adults created daily performances of learning without lesson plans or assessments and an international movement for social change that does not adhere to an ideology. As you read through the selections in this volume you will be introduced to these and many other activities, organizations and practices.

For Lois, the job of a methodologist is to continuously search for and create new tools that support, rather than explain, human development. She proposes that all of us become tool creators. She and Newman, borrowing from Vygotsky, created a term for this activity: tool-and-result methodology. In her 2011 talk "Fred Newman and the Search for Method" Lois contrasts tool-and-result with tool-for-result:

> When method is applied, the relation between tool and result is linear, instrumental and dualistic, or what Newman and I call tool for result methodology (Newman & Holzman, 1993). Vygotsky proposes a qualitatively different conception of method: not a tool to be applied, but an

activity (a "search") that generates both tool and result at the same time and as continuous process. Tool and result are not dualistically separated, nor are they identical, nor one thing. Rather, they are elements of a dialectical unity/totality/whole. Method to be practiced, not applied, is what Vygotsky was advocating.

One of the most provocative tool-and-result activities, and one that is the focus of a great deal of Lois' writing, is the practice of social therapy, a non-diagnostic, group approach to emotional development and therapy. Fred Newman created social therapy and practiced it for over 30 years, and he trained hundreds of other clinicians, many of them clinical social workers, psychologists or psychiatrists, in the approach. During almost all of this time Lois was Newman's collaborator, and in that role, she was his partner in social therapy's transformation from one of the many radical therapies that emerged out of the struggles for justice and equality of the 1960s (e.g., feminist and black psychology) into a practical-critical performatory methodology for reinitiating human development.

A unique strength Lois brought to the development/study of social therapy turned out to be that she herself is not a therapist! Lois looked at social therapy and saw its potential to create environments for development—not just in the therapy room, but everywhere. Over time the broader methodology of social therapeutics emerged, an approach that is now utilized in doctors' offices, outside-of-school youth programs, community organizing projects and in thousands of classrooms from preschool to graduate school. One of the key discoveries from social therapy is that the process of the group building/creating environments in which the group can develop (perform beyond themselves) is itself developmental. While social therapy may have emotional pain as its primary focus, the methodology of people in the group giving everything they have (including their pain, trauma and/or anger) to create the environment where people can grow offers powerful opportunities for development, learning, and community development and social change.

An example from practice. As educators, we have found Lois' writing on building environments for development to be of enormous value. It has given us new ways to understand what we are doing in our classrooms, and we use her articles and chapters to introduce our students, workshop participants and others to the methodology of social therapeutics and of relating to everyone as collective builders and meaning makers of environments.

One example of how this looks comes from my (Carrie's) work as a teacher educator, preparing mostly young women to be elementary and early childhood teachers in public schools in the United States.

My objective in my classes, in addition to teaching students the nuts and bolts of public school teaching, is to shift their gaze from solely acquiring (or teaching) content to being builders of environments where people can learn and develop. This is not easy! My students come into my classes after 16 years of learning how to be

Big Ideas and Revolutionary Activity

a student. They are eager to learn how to teach, but they know how to do that by being the recipients of knowledge. On the first day of class I share an observation made over years of teaching. "Most of you come into my classroom thinking about, wondering, or even worried about what it is that I, as the teacher, will make you do." I go on to say that this posture is deeply embedded in how teaching is understood and how schools are designed. "However," I say, "while you came to this class to learn how to be a teacher, I believe that to do that well you will have to rediscover how to be learners." Then I ask them, "How shall we do that together?"

This generates some confusion, awkwardness, occasional annoyance and ultimately quite a bit of curiosity. For 14 weeks, we try on different performances of learning. One week we spend the whole class generating questions without the need to answer them, another day groups self-organize to figure out how to learn things they have always wanted to know how to do. Sometimes the class even organizes me to lecture on a topic. While the activities vary, what remains the same is the focus on process and the willingness to challenge assumptions.

Lois' writings are useful throughout this process. My class and I explore what we think the relationship is between learning and development, and how they are inseparable in infancy and early childhood, but ripped apart once we enter school (See "Vygoskianizing Psychotherapy"). We examine play and performance and their relationship to creating environments where people can be both who they are and who they are becoming (See "Creating Communities of Hope" and "Play as if Your Mental Health Depended on It"). And we look at how creative imitation, completion and building zones of proximal development inspire children and adults alike to be co-creators of their learning (See "Without Creating ZPDs There Is No Creativity" and "Developmental Play for All"). In addition to being provoked by rigorous ideas, my students learn that it is the relationship between content and process that brings learning alive.

We share our understanding of methodologist and tool-and-result with you as one of several ways to understand who Lois is and also as an invitation for how to use this book. Lois does not write in order to give people a set of tools to use; she writes as an invitation to everyone to become methodologists. This is a challenge to how we usually read. We are taught to read in order to get answers, to agree or disagree with the author, and to decide what the best course of action is. Lois writes as an invitation to join her in the search for method. So, whether you are a community organizer, a researcher, a student, or a practitioner or someone who just likes new approaches and big ideas, as you go through the book, let yourself be inspired and use these chapters to inspire others to become tool makers and not just tool users, environment builders not just environment inhabitants, and to do so with others.

An Activist Scholar
Lois locates herself in the world as an activist. Over three decades ago, she began leading her life as a revolutionary and independent scholar, a change in location that

transformed what she could see and do. She is not driven by the need to publish to advance her career. Her scholarship is in the service of her efforts to change the world. Lois' intellectual and political commitment to not make a separation between research and practice has led her to pioneer new forms of research where the activity of doing the research is inseparable from the activities that she and the people around her are bringing into existence.

Within academia there are ongoing discussions about "bridging the divide" or "bringing research/theory and practice together." Lois' location as an activist scholar has transformed how she sees the "problem" of the relationship between research and practice—by challenging that there is a divide to bridge! As you read through this volume you will notice that, whether the content is social therapy, performance activism or diagnosis, and whatever form it takes, Lois locates her work as a member and builder of the communities and activities about which she is writing/researching. Her writing is inspired by the community building work that she and we are bringing into existence, and she is writing in no small part to continue to build that community.

Lois is an organizer who brings together people who do not usually converse. When she writes scholarly articles and books she introduces the academic world to the therapists, clients, inner city communities and international performance activists who are her collaborators. In her talks and blog posts she introduces the people who make up her community to the researchers and theorists whose work has such a big impact on their lives. Wherever Lois goes, whomever she is speaking to, whatever she is doing, she is standing with and talking with all people, not just the academics.

One example of her work as an organizer is her recent activities to bring the psychologists and psychiatrists who question the dominance of a medical model in mental health into conversation with the people who are impacted by this model. Through the implementation of a survey conducted at street fairs and online, and then through articles, blog posts, talks and classes, Lois and her colleagues have created an inclusive conversation on the impact of what she calls our "diagnostic way of life" (See The Diagnostic Debate: Voices from the Street and "A Diagnosis the DSM Forgot: Physics Envy").

Lois does not relate to anything as too complicated or abstract for the people of the world to engage. She challenges the assumption that it is necessary to have a certain kind of background, training, or degree to participate in playing with theory or in making discoveries. For example, for the past thirty years, Lois has been working to, as she describes it, "…bring Vygotsky from the scientific laboratory to ordinary people and their communities" (Holzman, 2017, p. 117). There is ample evidence to indicate that she is succeeding. Because of Lois, there are many more Vygotskians in the world today, and while many are in the university, many more are in the schools and streets of communities around the world. From the 19-year-old girl from East New York who speaks with ease about creating zones of proximal development, to

Big Ideas and Revolutionary Activity

the community organizers in Juarez, Mexico who have been sustained and inspired by Lois, Newman, and Vygotsky in the midst of horrific violence, to Syrian refugees who are playing and performing their way to a new culture and a more hopeful future, Lois has shared her methodology and passion with people all over world and they are using what she has given them to continue to create.

An example from practice. Elena Boukouvala is a drama and movement therapist and developmental psychologist who was taking her play and performance skills into challenging situations around the globe when she was introduced to Lois and the East Side Institute. In 2014 Elena participated in the Institute's International Class, a year-long immersion in social therapeutics that takes place under Lois' direction. During the course she further developed her understanding of the relationship between play, performance and human development and experienced firsthand Lois' leadership in the emerging international performance activism movement. In 2015 when refugees from Syria and other countries began pouring into her native country of Greece, Elena was an early responder.

Elena's first activities were to join with others who were bringing play and creative activities to young children in the camps, setting up play spaces and play days for hundreds of children and their caretakers. While volunteering with children in the camps Elena began meeting young adults who also wanted to play.

> I was in the camps playing with children and I was approached by young people who wanted to be part of the play. Mostly young adults—in their 20s—and the play that they wanted to create was more related to the community. They wanted to get out of the camps and create connections to people and to have an impact on the world. I was struck by how many people felt like creativity and being playful was a necessity. (E. Boukouvala, personal communication, March 5, 2017)

The people that Elena was meeting were eager to leave the camps and meet local artists. She began going with the refugees into the downtown areas of the city and introducing them to local artists and musicians. Over time they created a band made up of local and refugee musicians who created hybrid songs from their various countries of origins. They created environments where those who were called refugees and those who were called aid workers, volunteers or locals could create together in ways that were not completely determined by those categories.

> [A young refugee man] approached us and he did not ask for food or house, he asked to connect him to Greek musicians and to sing. I think that play became a way to respond and to create with the difficulties that people were experiencing. The violation of their human rights. It was like play became a revolution to that. (E. Boukouvala, personal communication, March 5, 2017)

Throughout human history there are many examples of beautiful and poignant art emerging out of crisis--Picasso's Guernica comes to mind. There has, however, been less discussion of the process of creating spaces where people who are in crisis and those who are supposed to be helping them can create art together. Bringing play into a situation like the refugee crisis in Europe makes a statement about who we are as human beings—we are not just victims, heroes, and villains—we are co-creators of the world and of our lives. And we are capable of creating new things together out of what is essentially "crap." As Elena says:

> The activity of creating culture has been alienated in our world. This also links to the work with play. We often assume that play belongs to children and culture belongs to artists. And this is [expletive]. Everyone can play and everyone can create culture. Just saying that is not enough, we need to create activities that challenge what people think play is and what people think culture is. How to transform that, and how to play with that, that is what we trying to do. (E. Boukouvala, personal communication, March 5, 2017)

Elena continues to develop as a leader of the growing performance activism movement internationally. She is bringing together activists, artists, scholars, and the growing groupings of people who have moved to Europe and are seeking to build a new life. And she is exploring the possibility of entering a PhD program. Like Lois she is bringing everything she has to organize people to build and create community and new performances of power together.

Seriously Playful

Lois' conceptualization of play (as performance) is inspired by the work of Vygotsky; she has taken play to places he never wrote about. Vygotsky saw play as the highest form of childhood development where children are both who they are and who they are becoming, referring to children's engagement with/in play as the activity of being "a head taller" than they are (Vygotsky, 1978, p. 102). Lois, in collaboration with Newman, was inspired and intrigued by this phrase "a head taller" and built upon/with Vygotsky's work on play and its possibilities for child development. Lois, and in this we consider ourselves her collaborators, has expanded this understanding of play in three important ways.

First, even when young children are not doing an activity that would be interpreted as play, they participate (without even knowing there is such a thing as participation), together with their caregivers, in creating environments where they can do things they have not yet learned how to do. Children are supported to walk, talk, wait for the bus, sit at the dinner table, use the toilet and an infinite number of other activities before knowing how to do any of these things and with little to no formal instruction. So for very young children there is no rigid separation between play and work/instruction.

A second way that Lois has helped expand on Vygotsky's understanding of play is to take his discoveries beyond the realm of early childhood. Play does not disappear

Big Ideas and Revolutionary Activity

after early childhood--being who you are and who you are not is a lifespan activity. Adults use this ability when they pretend to be the baby when playing with their children, or in creating an avatar of themselves in an online game. And, like babies and toddlers, older children and adults also utilize this ability when they are not officially playing. For example, adults are both "who they are and who they are becoming" when they start a new job or become a parent for the first time.

However, while we can continue to play we are rarely encouraged to do so. When early childhood and its socially-sanctioned play activities end children are sent the message that it is time to stop playing and stick to discovering/being who you are. This often means that people stop doing what they do not know how to do and learning and development suffer. This leads to the final, and perhaps most consequential advance that Lois has helped make to Vygotsky's theory, which is to call attention to the relationship between play, as described above, and performance. Performance is the word that is given to the socially sanctioned activity of being who you are and who you are not after early childhood.

Lois has spent decades teaching that performance is too valuable an activity to be left only to professional actors and small children. It is by being supported to be who you are and who you are not that older children and adults can continue to develop. From this perspective, development is understood, not as a set of stages that a person passes through on their way to adulthood, but as the collective creation of stages (environments) where everyone can perform who they are becoming.

And, of course, as we hope is abundantly clear by now, Lois does not talk about play and performance as a purely intellectual activity. She is continuously developing projects and creating environments where people of all ages play and perform their way to development. One example of this is the biennial Performing the World (PTW) conferences that Lois initiated in 2001. The motivation for the conference came in part from Lois' international travels where she was meeting increasing numbers of people who were using performance for personal and social change. Most of these people were working in isolation, unaware that there were others making similar discoveries.

The East Side Institute, led by Lois, created PTW as a playground for these innovators, who were joined by hundreds of others including community organizers, helping professionals, academics and many others to come together for three days of intellectual, theatrical, therapeutic and political play. PTW is more than a conference or a showcase. It has become a community and an emerging movement (See "Performing the World: The Performance Turn in Social Activism"). One way to understand the founding of PTW is that Lois related to the people she was meeting as performing a head taller than they were—as builders of a new kind of social movement. And PTW has become the stage that we are collectively building to bring the performance activism movement into existence.

Lois' conceptualization of play as performance, then, invites us to build groups and the environments we would like to have in order to grow. In doing so, this approach challenges familiar and common notions of play as "recess" or "a warm up to or release from the 'real' work," or performance as "what only actors/artists do." Her conceptualization of performance becomes the means of co-creating activities and environments that support and embrace lifespan, ongoing development for all people/communities/systems. It is our continual ability to perform collectively that transcends familiar and traditional views of development that adopt deterministic and acquisitional lenses on environments/activities/people. Lois' writings, as articulate, sophisticated, and interdisciplinary as they are, are only part of the inspiration and power of Lois' work. What emerges from Lois' work is a call to perform/enact/embody/realize them in the world—not have them remain as ideas on a page to be read and discussed, but more so as a call to action.

An example from practice. In our workshops at the East Side Institute we often have participants with a wide range of experiences (e.g., as psychologists, artists, and community activists) and educational backgrounds (e.g., people with doctorates and people who did not complete secondary school). They arrive at our workshops with very different degrees of preparation to engage with complex or sophisticated texts, and in particular those like Lois' that challenge the understandings of learning and development that are common in the world. So, our task as we see it is to help them create a collective performance of learning, one where everyone can participate.

One way that we support that is to invite the participants to take sections of a text by Lois that intrigues or confuses them and have them create poems with the words in these sections. Following Lois' understanding of language as a meaning-making activity, we have found that people can make meaning together when they break from the usual activity of reading primarily for information. We have them take words from the reading and rearrange them to see how they can give articulation to the words in another way/form. What follows is a poem collectively created by a group of online workshop participants.

Development
colonialistic history—progression, improvement...
and yet...
Discovery and building
a force for change
transformation that allows us to understand ourselves
and our world,
to make sense of our lives
Discovering and creating
new performances, new activities, new emotions, new learning and
to do this socially
with others
To question and rethink in process...
free of proofing or defining
A dynamic human process
change and transformation

Big Ideas and Revolutionary Activity

shaped by and shaping
the environment in which it takes place.
Looking, not linearly or as spectrums but as much more
complex networks/rhizomes
with ideas not reflecting
but diffracting
multiple different directions and different possibilities.
"Is development always growth?"

The conceptualization of the collective performance offers us to become co-creators of what/how/why we engage in the building and developing of the group. To do so, Lois's work has been extremely helpful and transformative. In effect, Lois' work transforms our performance of simply/only being "professors" or "students" or, for example, "doctors" and "patients" or "refugees" and "aid workers" to becoming revolutionary co-builders of environments that are holistic, radically inclusive, relational, seriously playful and continuously created with/in the dialectics of process/product and being/becoming.

In light of this and our other examples from practice, we invite you, in the spirit in which Lois has intended, to engage with her work in deep and integrated ways. We see Lois' writings as a call to action: to use the selections in this book in the spirit that they are written: offer(s) of a new methodology. And so, we invite you to use the work to teach/create/build with others with/in a new methodology.

Overview of the Book

We are excited to share the big ideas and revolutionary activity that Lois writes of/co-creates/inspires with and in the contents of this book. As Lois' written work spans many contexts, disciplines and communities it does also with respect to the forms it takes. The variety of forms is essential to honoring who Lois is and her invitation to make possible human development and social and community change: there is a host of ways to do so, and everyone is invited and included to build them. That said, we have selected important and timely book chapters, articles, talks and blog posts by Lois that reflect her community building and search for method with/in play, performance activism, social therapy, diagnosis and community building. The texts are introduced and organized into three sections: chapters and articles first, talks second and blog posts third. Texts within each section are presented from first to most recently published. For the sections with chapters/articles and talks, an introduction to each text precedes it. For the third section, an overview of the blog posts introduces you to the topics Lois covers in them. We invite you to explore, connect, build with and share them, and in doing so, search for the method(s) to perform and create big ideas and revolutionary activity with/in your communities.

References

Fred Newman, PhD. (2013). Retrieved from http://frednewmanphd.com/about-fred-newman.

Holzman, L. (2011, October). *Fred Newman and the search for method*. Paper presented at The Third International Academic Conference on Contemporary Capitalism Studies, Hangzhou, China.

Holzman, L. (2017). *Vygotsky at work and play*. London and New York: Routledge. (Original work published 2009).

Holzman, L. (2018). *The overweight brain: How our obsession with knowing keeps us from getting smart enough to make a better world*. New York: East Side Institute.

Newman, F. & Holzman, L. (1996). *Unscientific psychology: A cultural performatory approach to understanding human life*. Westport, CT: Praeger.

Newman, F. & Holzman, L. (2006). *The end of knowing*. London: Routledge.

Newman, F. & Holzman, L. (2013). *Lev Vygotsky: Revolutionary scientist (classic edition)*. New York: Psychology Press. (Original work published 1993).

Vygotsky, L. (1978). *Mind in society*. Cambridge, MA: Harvard University Press.

Big Ideas and Revolutionary Activity

Articles and Chapters

Big Ideas and Revolutionary Activity

Ludwig Wittgenstein, The Tortured Smarty Pants

A World Class Thinker Who Taught Us the Dangers of Knowing

Ludwig Wittgenstein, The Tortured Smarty Pants: A World Class Thinker Who Taught Us the Dangers of Knowing introduces readers to Lois's relationship to Ludwig Wittgenstein, an influential, yet little known (outside of philosophy departments) philosopher of the 20th century. Born in 1889, Wittgenstein lived a difficult life, some even go so far as to say a tortured one. In his first book, *Tractatus Logico-Philosophicus*, he claimed to have solved all philosophical problems through a logical approach to language and meaning and how they relate to the world. In his next book, *Philosophical Investigations*, he openly admitted that he had been wrong, stating that language cannot be pinned down or presented systematically, asserting that the act of thinking of language in this way is the very thing that creates problems and confusion. Lois asserts that we have been conditioned to think and speak dualistically, in terms of either this, or that. We have also come to believe that words mirror the world and that they have an attachment to something that exists "out there." Wittgenstein suggests the way out is not to assume but to look. By questioning our assumptions, we widen our view, seeing things we've never seen before.

One of the books on my Kindle is *The First Scientific American, Benjamin Franklin and the Pursuit of Genius* by Harvard historian Joyce Chaplin. It's an intellectual biography of one of the most famous and influential signers of the Declaration of Independence and the US Constitution. Franklin was also a career politician, scientist, inventor,

Big Ideas and Revolutionary Activity

philosopher, printer, writer and shrewd entrepreneur. I've long been intrigued by all he is said to have accomplished and how he came to have so much fame. Chaplin's book fills in the blanks. I've gotten to know Ben Franklin for sure. More than that, I've learned how public scientific and philosophical discoveries and debates were in the 1700s, through publication in pamphlets, periodicals and newspapers that anyone who could read had access to.

Which brings us to Ludwig Wittgenstein. The most influential philosopher of the 20th century, he's obviously seriously studied by philosophers. And Wittgenstein is also well known in broader intellectual circles, with tens of thousands of articles and books written about his work (100 new books just since 2000, according to the British Wittgenstein Society), and stage plays, poems and films about his life being performed. His thinking is like no other before or since, and he lived a highly unusual life—the public would be fascinated to know of him. And yet the person on the street (who's heard of Plato) never heard of Wittgenstein. Had he lived at a time when philosophy and science were in the public domain, I wonder if he might be as famous as Ben Franklin.

Ludwig Wittgenstein was born in 1889, lived through two World Wars, the Russian Revolution, and the beginning of the Cold War (he died in 1953). He led a conflicted (some biographers go so far as to say tortured) life. He was Austrian and spent his early years in Vienna, but became a British citizen as an adult. He lived for varying amounts of time in both urban and rural areas in nearly a dozen other countries, with Cambridge England the home he would return to. He was the youngest of eight children, three of whom committed suicide. His family was cultured, influential and extremely wealthy, and he gave away his portion of the inheritance to his siblings and lived with minimal means. His mother was partly Jewish and three of his four great grandparents had converted and changed their names (to comply with the 1808 Napoleonic decree that Jews must adopt a Christian surname), and raised their children as Catholics. However, the family was considered Jewish when Hitler came to power. Attracted for a period of his youth to some anti-Semitic and homophobic writings, as an adult he expressed worry and moral confusion about his homosexuality, his Jewishness, the nature of sin, and a self-imposed obligation to live a meaningful and moral life. He hated the pomposity and isolation of the academic ivory tower, yet could be as pompous and exclusionary as his stuffy colleagues. Other philosophers were in awe of his brilliance, even struggling to understand his lectures and manuscripts—and he himself was crazy about "low brow" art like American musicals and dime store detective novels. Perhaps the event that captures best his unusual nature was his public denunciation of his own early and brilliant philosophical writings and their "old ways of thinking." (See Note 1 for ways to learn more about Wittgenstein).

I Was Wrong

It was his *Tractatus Logico-Philosophicus*, published in 1919, which Wittgenstein later rejected. The slim and unusual book—only 75 pages long and written as a series of hierarchically numbered sentences, the *Tractatus* (as it is usually referred to) claimed to solve all the problems of philosophy through a logical approach to language and meaning, and their relationship to the stuff of the world. With logic as the guide, or god, the social, interactive and cultural nature of language and meaning was ignored. Over the next twenty years or so, Wittgenstein became more and more uncomfortable with his own narrow and dogmatic thinking. In the opening pages to his next book, *Philosophical Investigations*, he commented that in re-reading the *Tractatus*, "I have been forced to recognize grave mistakes in what I wrote in that first book." *Philosophical Investigations* is a collection of thoughts, he wrote, that go off in many directions. They can't be pinned down or presented systematically.

And neither can language—that's the message of *Philosophical Investigations*. (He never published this book; others did so after he died). In this book Wittgenstein tries to show how thinking of language as logical and systematic is the very thing that creates philosophical problems and everyday confusion in our thinking and our communication with one another. Put another way, Wittgenstein went from delineating how language is thoroughly knowable to trying to show how it is **not knowable**. Further, he went from proclaiming the ideas in the *Tractatus* to be "truth unassailable" to writing that *Philosophical Investigations* was "only an album." You've got to admire him.

I'm a Wittgensteinian. Fred Newman introduced me to him more than twenty-five years ago. I immediately was taken, but so awed by him and by Fred's understanding of him that it's taken me a very long time to feel as close to Wittgenstein as I do to Vygotsky. There's still a distance, but I'm getting there. (See Note 2 for Newman on Wittgenstein).

Wittgenstein's Puzzles

I find Wittgenstein's style of writing fun to read and an incredible challenge to understand. Whatever I do comprehend, I suspect, owes a lot to how he writes what he writes. He presents us with puzzles and invites us into the process of solving them.

Here's one of his puzzles

We call many different things games (there're card games and board games and ball games and Olympic games, and more). Is there something common to all of them? Is there "an essence of game"? After posing this, Wittgenstein writes, "Don't say: "There *must* be something common, or they would not be called 'games.'—but **look and see** whether there is anything common to all." If you look, he writes, you won't see anything common to all of them; instead you'll see many different similarities and relationships between this kind of game and that kind, and between that kind and another kind, and so on. If you look, the "problem" vanishes. What's the problem, you ask? The problem is that we impose a false logic upon our language activity—we think that language is systematic and consistent and since we call these things games, there must be some characteristic that they share, some abstract "game-ness."

Big Ideas and Revolutionary Activity

But language doesn't work that way. It's a creative human cultural-social activity. Words don't get their meaning from the dictionary. They don't get their meaning from the things they name. What confuses us is our belief that if a word means something there must be an object it corresponds to. For example, we'd all agree that the word "addiction" has meaning. But it's quite another thing (or, it should be, Wittgenstein tells us) to believe that therefore there must be some thing that the word "addiction" corresponds to. People create meaning through speaking together, through using words (along with tones of voice and gestures and body language) in all kinds of ways in all kinds of situations and relationships. "Addiction" means one thing in a conversation about your puppy and his favorite toy, but it means quite another thing in a conversation at a rehab center. You're playing one "language game" and the folks at the rehab center are playing another. But to the extent that we misunderstand what language is and take meaning to be fixed and language to mirror the world, we confuse ourselves and get into conversational standoffs (or worse, fights).

What all this has to do with knowing and growing is—everything! How we understand what language is has everything to do with how we use language, how we talk to ourselves and to one another, and—and this may surprise you—how we think and what we think about. Nearly all of Wittgenstein's "puzzles" expose how both—our speaking and our thinking—presume everything is knowable. He had a powerful image for how the way we speak narrows our thinking in this way: "A picture held us captive. And we could not get outside it, for it lay in our language and language seemed to repeat it to us inexorably." (See Note 3 for the source of this quote).

If you doubt being "held captive," think of the Wittgenstein puzzle I shared earlier about trying to find what's common to all games (a picture of everything having an "essence"). Or assuming "addiction" refers to some thing that exists (a picture of words corresponding to things). Or the last conversation you were involved in that was framed as either/or—maybe it was about someone or something being good or bad; or sexuality being biological or social; or some person's action, behavior or personality stemming from "nature" or from "nurture"; or whether someone's sickness was "all in their head" or "real" (either mind or body). We frame conversations with either/or. We speak either/or and we think either/or. We operate as if words mean "this" and that "this" means "NOT that." Either/or is one of the pictures that hold us captive, and it lies in our language.

Our language and the pictures it creates, Wittgenstein tells and shows us in his writing, gets us into intellectual–emotional muddles, like feeling forced to choose nature or nurture. Without even thinking about it we look for the essences and causes of things, and for interpretations and explanations for our thoughts and our words. It creates confusion. We find ourselves stuck in traps and narrow spaces. It torments and bewilders us. It gives us "mental cramps." It makes us sick.

Can We Escape?

Luckily, there's a cure for this sickness. Here's how Wittgenstein describes it:

What I do is suggest, or even invent, other ways of looking at it. I suggest possibilities of which you had not previously thought. You thought that there was one possibility, or only two at most. But I made you think of others. Furthermore, I made you see that it was absurd to expect the concept to conform to those narrow possibilities. Thus, your mental cramp is relieved, and you are free to look around the field of use of the expression and to describe the different kinds of uses of it. (See Note 4 for the source of this quote).

The cure, he is saying, is to not assume but to look. To investigate our assumptions, widen our view, see things we've never seen before, and admit possibilities. To play with our language, look at how people actually speak with one another, open our eyes and ears and see all the many ways we use words. To expose how narrow, rigid and institutionalized our language and understanding of language has been. To see the activity of creating meaning together and that we cannot know what anything means until we create it. To embrace that we cannot know, but that we can create.

I think what Wittgenstein was trying to do was profound and is, more than ever, profoundly needed. He was trying to show the ways that language obscures life-as-lived and to give us a way to be less alienated from *what we do*. His work focused on the language created by philosophy and psychology because it's those languages that do a lot of the obscuring. Psychology's concerns and conceptions—personality, identity, the self, the mind, mental illness, cognition, emotions, intelligence, prejudice, language, talent, abnormality—these terms are spoken and written about as if there are specific things in the world they correspond to. Psychologists claim to know not only what they are, but also how they're made and what caused them and where to "find" them (the current fad being to place them somewhere in the brain). It seems to me that psychology has a sickness in Wittgenstein's sense—it thing-ifies, systematizes and essentializes everything. It's addicted (excuse the expression) to knowing. And that holds us captive.

Like Vygotsky, Wittgenstein gives us a way to understand language as a form of human life, a social creative activity that continuously creates culture. While their life journeys could not have been more different, they came to some similar places about how thinking and speaking make us human. And it's not what you might think.

What is the relation between thinking (and feeling) and speaking? You probably haven't stayed awake pondering this question. But I guarantee there's an "operating principle" at play as you go about your daily life thinking and feeling and speaking. That principle goes something like this: "I have a thought or a feeling and my words express what it is. Sometimes I get it right and sometimes I don't."

It's this way of picturing thinking and speaking that deprives us of our humanity, according to both Vygotsky and Wittgenstein. For our humanity lies in our social-

Big Ideas and Revolutionary Activity

ness, in our activity and in our capacity to create. We don't **express** what we're thinking or feeling when we speak. We don't find the words that match and say them. Speaking isn't finding a correspondence for either something material or psychological. It's not a read out of some inner life that we lead. This expressionist picture of language is wrong, Wittgenstein says. Speaking is the social activity of creating and playing what he called "language games" (there's that "game" again):

"The *speaking* of language is part of an activity, or of a form of life." (See Note 5 for the source of this quote). Vygotsky filled in this **new picture** with these words: "The structure of speech is not simply the mirror image of the structure of thought. It cannot, therefore, be placed on thought like clothes off a rack. Thought is restructured as it is transformed into speech. It is not expressed but completed in the word." (See Note 6 for the source of this quote).

I like to imagine that Wittgenstein would have lots to say to Vygotsky about thought being completed in the word, but these two great thinkers never met in real life. Fortunately, they're characters in some of Fred Newman's plays. There's one play in particular— *The Myth of Psychology*—in which their relationship comes alive as they seek therapy for help with their relationship. It's one of my favorite Newman plays. I think it will help make clearer what their smartness, their revolutionariness, their love, their passion and their torment have contributed to the world—and I invite you to read it. (See Note 7 for more about this play and where you can find the script).

Notes to Help You Go Broader and Deeper

1. *Ray Monk's Ludwig Wittgenstein: The Duty of Genius* is a terrific biography that weaves together Wittgenstein's life and idea histories. It's nearly 700 pages, but reads (almost) like a novel. The Brechtian (I call it edu-taining) film "Wittgenstein" by the late Derek Jarman is on You Tube. The best version is the entire film in one piece, with Spanish subtitles, at https://www.youtube.com/watch?v=Ilu70Jo38eo. Among the many video of philosophers discussing Wittgenstein's work, I like both the sensibility and accessibility of "Philosophy as Therapy: Wittgenstein" https://www.youtube.com/watch?v=gUGLKMOeqLE In terms of reading Wittgenstein himself, after playing with Philosophical Investigations, browse through *Remarks on the Philosophy of Psychology*.

2. Fred Newman felt very, very close to Wittgenstein. He loved to share with anyone who was interested what Wittgenstein's unhappiness with philosophy was, what his concerns were, what he discovered and what he didn't discover. Always Fred did this personally and historically, bringing relevance and dramatic flair to the topic. One widely read essay, entitled "A Therapeutic Deconstruction of the Illusion of Self," appears in my 1999 book, *Performing Psychology: A Postmodern Culture of the Mind. The End of Knowing and Unscientific Psychology*, which Fred and I wrote together, are other good sources.

3. This quotation from Wittgenstein appears in *Philosophical Investigations*, paragraph 115. (Most citations from published works give the page numbers of the publication, but the convention for Wittgenstein's writings is to cite the paragraph by its number instead of the page).

4. This quotation from Wittgenstein appears in the Monk biography I recommended above, on page 502.

5. This quotation and more on language-games appears in *Philosophical Investigations*, paragraph 23.

6. This quotation from Vygotsky appears in *The Collected Works of L. S. Vygotsky, Volume 1*, on page 251.

7. Fred Newman wrote 44 plays. In most of them he had people from different historical periods and those who never met (like Wittgenstein and Vygotsky) meet and talk. Only the first act of Newman's play *The Myth of Psychology* appears in print— with the title *Beyond the Pale*. It's included in the collection of Newman plays up to 1998 edited by Dan Friedman, entitled *Still on the Corner and Other Postmodern Political Plays by Fred Newman*. It also appears in Newman's and my book *The End of Knowing*. Fred wrote *Beyond the Pale* for a live performance at the American Psychological Association Annual Meeting in 1996. It was a big hit and, for some years after, this annual gathering of many thousands of psychologists scheduled a live performance of a specially written Newman play among its sessions—including one of a second meeting of Vygotsky, Wittgenstein and the therapist.

Wittgenstein is a character in other Newman plays. In *Life Upon the Wicked Stage*, a very young Wittgenstein converses first with Franz Kafka and then with Sigmund Freud. And then there's *Outing Wittgenstein*—a wonderfully funny play in which Wittgenstein and his gay alter ego appear on the TV show, "This is Your Death." (You'll find both play scripts in Friedman's *Still on the Corner*).

Big Ideas and Revolutionary Activity

Relating to People as Revolutionaries

Relating to People as Revolutionaries means relating to people as socio-cultural-history makers in their everyday life activity, even within the most mundane moments of life. By revealing and fostering our capacity to be both who we are and who we are becoming, social therapeutics empowers us to perform beyond ourselves. It reminds us of our human capacity to change totalities and create new and revolutionary ways of being and doing. Social therapeutics was created in the 1970s by a group of activists working with the poorest communities in New York City. Since that time, it has emerged as a methodology for human development and learning, therapeutics, community building and social change that is practiced all over the world. This methodology is deeply philosophical and theoretically grounded, and it is immensely practical. Social therapeutics embraces the dynamics that our intersectionalities (i.e., race, gender, sexuality, class and intellectual ability) bring to the stage and encourages us to create something new together. Its emphasis on the group or "groupness" allows its members to produce new meaning collectively, qualitatively transforming what is into what can be, together.

What do you do in your moments of despair upon hearing or seeing the latest horror human beings have inflicted upon each other—in your own neighborhood or thousands of miles away from it? Sometimes, what happens for me is a certain phrase or two will "pop into my head" and ground me, by which I mean allow me to locate the horrific events in the contradictory totality of human history and its dialectic with human society, in the human capacity to continuously overthrow (re-create) that which we have created. One of these phrases is a quote from the Soviet psychologist Lev Vygotsky: "A revolution solves only those tasks raised by history" (Vygotsky, quoted in frontispiece, Levitin, 1982). Another is from French cultural theorist Sylvère Lotringer: "One does not cure neurosis, one changes a society which cannot do without it" (1977). And a third was spoken by Dr. Martin Luther King, Jr.: "The salvation of our world lies in the hands of the maladjusted" (King, 1956, 27 June 1956 address to the Annual Convention of the NAACP in San Francisco, http://www.mindfreedom.org/kb/mental-health-global/iaacm/MLK-on-IAACM). Each of these propositions speaks to me in the performative—"Don't mourn, organize!" They convey not a critical but a *practical-critical* approach to the therapy professions.

In 2003 Fred Newman and I wrote an article entitled, "All Power to the Developing," that appeared in the *Annual Review of Critical Psychology*. There we presented a picture of our practical-critical psychotherapy by foregrounding its debt to Marx's radical humanism—by which we meant his insistence on the sociality of human beings and,

Big Ideas and Revolutionary Activity

in particular, his conception of revolutionary activity. In our discussion of social therapy, which was created by Newman in the 1970s, we focused on its activity of relating to all people as revolutionaries: "Relating to patients as revolutionaries entails relating to them as world historic in everyday, mundane matters, that is, as social beings engaged in the life/history-making process of always *becoming* (assimilating "all the wealth of previous development"). For what is history/making history if it is not the dialectic what is/what is becoming?" (Newman & Holzman, 2003, p.11).

This feature of social therapy was first articulated in a 1986 speech by Newman to the Congress of the Interamerican Society of Psychology, held in the Karl Marx Theater in Havana, Cuba. The following quote says more of what we mean by relating as revolutionaries:

> We speak of social therapy as revolution for non-revolutionaries. This radical Marxist conception – that the fundamental or essential human characteristic is being capable of carrying out revolutionary activity (what Marx calls practical-critical activity)—that's the foundation of anything which can be called or should be called a Marxist psychology. Ours is a radical insistence that we not accommodate reactionary society by relating to people—*any* people—as anything but revolutionaries. (Newman, 1991, p.15; Newman & Holzman, 2003, pp. 11-12)

It is now 2014, nearly 30 years since the Havana speech and more than a decade since the article "All Power..." appeared. Over these years, Newman and I continued to work together until he passed away in 2011—organizing, writing and expanding social therapy practices as well as other environments and activities that relate to people as revolutionaries. The methodology of social therapy (social therapeutics) has broadened to education, health care, youth work and organizational development. In the past decade the chasm that existed between theoretical critical psychology and alternative practices in psychology and psychotherapy has begun to blur. New critical practices have developed, and, to some extent, this has advanced the overall substance and quality of the intellectual conversation. The debate continues, but critique and practice are now closer together. At the same time, the bureaucracy and institutionalization of the helping professions of psychology, counseling, social work, psychiatry and psychotherapy have become more oppressive and harder and harder to get around. The medical and natural science models of understanding and relating to human beings are so dominant that non-mainstream approaches are rarely taught in universities or professional schools and the options available to those seeking help are becoming more and more limited. The work continues.

This article is an invitation to go beyond the critical to create practical-critical psychotherapy and counseling approaches.

Origins of Social Therapy

Social therapy originated in the 1970s as part of the social-cultural change movements of the time, which tied the "personal" to the political. It was developed by a community of activists who began by working in the poorest communities of New York City and has since gone on to organize middle class and wealthy people to support poor people to develop and provide leadership to the process of positive social change, free of government, corporate or university dependence. In this organizing process, new kinds of relationships are created between rich and poor, and all develop emotionally, socially and culturally. This organizing has led to international training in the social therapeutic methodology, the development of outside-of-school youth programs, a free of charge developmental learning center for inner-city youth and adults, a political theatre, a research and training center, an emergent international movement of performance activists, independent electoral campaigns, and partnerships with organizations on a national and international stage. With this significant quantitative and qualitative expansion over the decades, the inseparability of human development from community development has become more and more obvious.

Central to all the activities, organizations and projects of this activist community is an understanding of the necessity of affording opportunities for all people to engage in the practical-critical activity of creating their own development—in other words, of relating to people as revolutionaries. The mode of relating is performatory, grounded in the discovery that performing (as the "always becoming" activity) is what allows human beings to develop beyond instinctual and socially patterned behavior.

Similar to other new psychologies springing up at the time, social therapy was ideology based—in the belief that living under capitalism makes people emotionally sick and in the hope that therapy could be a tool in the service of progressive politics. Like the radical therapies of the 1970s, social therapy engaged the authoritarianism, sexism, racism, classism and homophobia of traditional psychotherapy. But social therapy's unique feature, even in its earliest years, was its engagement of the philosophical underpinnings of psychology and psychotherapy. It rejected explanation, interpretation, the notion of an inner self that therapists and clients need to delve into, and other dualistic and problematic foundations of traditional psychology. These are characteristics of what are now known as postmodern psychologies (e.g., Gergen, 1991; Gergen & Gergen, 2012; Holzman & Morss, 2000; Kvale, 1992).

As an emerging practical-critical epistemological and ontological critique, social therapy was influenced by Newman's study of Marxian dialectics and the philosophy of science and language (Wittgenstein's work in particular), and my study of human development, psycholinguistics and Vygotsky, and work as a qualitative researcher. Their methodological innovations helped us to see the potential for ordinary people to effect radical social change and to better understand the subjective constraints that need to be engaged so as to actualize this potential (e.g., Holzman, 2006; Newman & Holzman, 2006/1996; 2003). In particular, we read Marx and Vygotsky

Big Ideas and Revolutionary Activity

as valuable contributors to dissolving the dualist gap between self and world, between thought and language, between who we are and who we are becoming, and between theory and practice, in such a way that it becomes possible to approach human beings as activists and activity-ists, not as knowers and perceivers.

Unpacking Marx

In actualizing Marx's dialectic understanding of history/making history in the service of supporting people to perform as revolutionaries, we had to "postmodernize Marx." Ironically, we find the seeds for such postmodernization in Marx's own work (his earliest, most philosophical writings rather than his later work on political economy). Marx was no psychologist and didn't particularly address psychological issues, but he was nevertheless a fine critical psychologist. In the *Economic and Political Manuscripts* and *The German Ideology*, for example, Marx speaks clearly about the social nature, i.e., the ontology—of human activity and of human development.

> … *as* society itself produces *man* as *man*, so it is *produced* by him. Activity and mind are social in their content as well as in their *origin*; they are *social* activity and *social* mind. (Marx, 1967, p.129)

This is as clear a rejection of the dualisms of the mental and the physical, thought and action, and the individual and the social upon which psychology is based as I have ever read.

> We have further shown that private property can be abolished only on condition of an all-round development of individuals, because the existing character of intercourse and productive forces is an all-round one, and only individuals that are developing in an all-round fashion can appropriate them, i.e., can turn them into free manifestations of their lives. (Marx & Engels, 1974, p. 117)

Here we have a rejection of the psychological understanding of human development and the field of psychology's claim to investigate and come to understand it. Development does not happen to us, unfolding in a pre-determined progression of stages toward some end. For Marx, development is "all-round." All-round development is revolutionary, practical-activity. This social, communal and reconstructive activity of human beings exercising their power to transform the current state of things is what makes individual and species development possible (Holzman, 2009; Newman & Holzman, 2013/1993, 2003).

These passages from Marx presage contemporary postmodern concerns with psychological and psychotherapeutic methods that are premised on *individuals*, that is, entities which exist in social surrounds but are not themselves social; and *development* as a characteristic of such entities, specifically, of particular aspects or parts of such entities.

Social therapy is an actualization of the above critique. First, its focus, meaning the work of the therapist and the group—no matter the size, i.e., a group of 2 (therapist and client) or a group of 30—is the activity of the social unit developing. By engaging in this new kind of activity of creating their group, people are simultaneously creating who they are/are becoming, emotionally speaking. Such a focus on development is rare in the psychotherapy world, which focuses on "curing" the individual, relieving her/his symptoms, or some other form of correction of something presumed to be internally faulty and causing problematic outward manifestations.

Second, emotions in social therapy are not understood as products or possessions of individuals or as something internal that is made manifest in outward behavior, but rather as social, relational activity ("social activity and social mind"). In social therapy, the group is working to exercise its power to overthrow—to the extent possible under current political, economic and socio-cultural conditions—the alienation and commodification necessary for everyday life, including the professional and everyday psychological understanding of what emotions are and where they "reside."

Social therapy is most often conducted in groups and it is not the individual members of the group, but the group itself that is the therapeutic unit. This is different from most group therapies, in which the group serves as a context for the therapist to help individuals with their emotional problems. Clients who come together to form a social therapy group are given the task to create their group as an environment in which they can get help. This group activity is a collective, practical challenge to the assumption that the way people get therapeutic help is to relate to themselves and be related to by others as individuals, complete with problems and with inner selves.

In the US-based centers for social therapy, groups range in size from 8-30 people, a mix of women and men of varying ages, ethnicities, sexual orientations, class backgrounds and economic status, professions and "presenting problems." This heterogeneity is designed to challenge people's notion of a fixed identity (e.g., based on gender, ethnicity, diagnostic label, or "That's the kind of person I am"), and to maximize the diversity of "material" the group has to create with. Groups are typically 90 minutes long and meet weekly in an ongoing basis. Some group members remain for years, others months; people leave and new members join. The therapeutic environment and its potential "building material" is thus in continuous flux.

In a sense, each social therapy group is working to re-locate itself in history while remaining in society. For we all live in that dialectic. But we don't experience it. Most people do not experience their world-historicalness; they experience only their societal location (e.g., temporal, spatial and cultural). Our social identities are versions of the many ways there are to be alienated, commodified, separated and objectified. Our historical identity is as revolutionaries, as social, cultural, historical creators of something new out of what exists.

Big Ideas and Revolutionary Activity

The many hundreds of practitioners trained in social therapy who work in institutionalized settings modify their practices accordingly. Additionally, in other countries, social therapy is practiced in a structure and manner that is coherent with the specifics of the given cultural environments.

Vygotsky's Contribution

Vygotsky has been invaluable to our understanding the contemporary relevance of Marx's radical historical humanism just discussed, and to the continued development of our practical-critical psychotherapy (Holzman, 2009, 2013; Newman & Holzman, 2014/1993). During the revolutionary times of the early 20th century when both the first communist state and the new discipline of psychology were beginning, Vygotsky saw his task as that of having to create *a new kind of method* (method as dialectical activity) in order to study psychological activity and create a new psychology that would be coherent with and support the development of a new kind of society: "The search for method becomes one of the most important problems of the entire enterprise of understanding the uniquely human forms of psychological activity. In this case, the method is simultaneously prerequisite and product, the tool and the result of the study" (Vygotsky, 1978, p. 65).

Here Vygotsky is suggesting a radical break with the accepted scientific paradigm in which method is a tool that is applied and yields results. There, the relation between tool and result is linear, instrumental and dualistic (coined *tool-for-result methodology* in Newman & Holzman, 2014/1993). Vygotsky's "search" is a qualitatively different conception of method— not a tool to be applied, but an activity that generates both tool and result at the same time and as continuous process. Tool and result are not dualistically separated, neither are they the same or one thing. Rather, they are elements of a dialectical unity/totality/whole. Method to be practiced, not applied, is what Vygotsky was advocating. To capture the dialectical relationship of this new conception, Newman and I called this *tool-and-result methodology* (Newman & Holzman, 2014/1993). Importantly, this new conception of method is neither objective nor subjective, but something outside that dualistic box.

In addition to proposing a qualitatively new way to study human life, Vygotsky is pointing to the dialectical nature of human development and how to re-initiate it if it has been stopped. For human beings are not only tool users but also tool makers. We do not merely respond to stimuli, acquire societally determined and useful skills, and adapt to the determining environment. The uniqueness of human social life is that we ourselves transform the determining circumstances. Human development is not an individual accomplishment but a *socio-cultural activity*.

Understanding Vygotsky's conception of method as dialectical tool-and-result provided a new way of seeing social therapy, namely, as the group's activity of creating itself as the tool-and-result of their (becoming) emotional development. We identified Vygotsky as a forerunner to "a new psychology of becoming," in which people experience the social nature of their existence and the power of collective creative activity in the process of making new tools (-and-results) for growth (Holzman, 2009). Relating to people as revolutionaries is akin, we came to believe, to relating to them as tool-and-result makers/methodologists/practical-critical dialecticians.

Further Vygotskian insights followed from this methodological one. For example, his understanding of the role of play in early childhood remains today unique and uniquely dialectical. "In play a child always behaves beyond his average age, above his daily behavior; in play it is as though he were a head taller than himself" (Vygotsky, 1978, p. 102). We took this as a metaphor for the being/becoming dialectic of human development and expanded it to adolescence and adulthood. Recognizing that performers on stage are also simultaneously who they are and the characters they are playing, we came to understand performance as a Vygotskian kind of play, and to understand that human beings perform our development. This became not only the topic of our subsequent investigations and writings but simultaneously the direction our practices and those of our colleagues took in therapy as well in educational, organizational and cultural settings (Friedman, 2011; Holzman, 1997, 2009; Holzman & Newman, 2012; Lobman, 2011; Martinez, 2011; Newman & Holzman, 1997, 2006/1996).

In order for social therapy participants to create their therapy group and simultaneously create new emotional activity, they must *perform therapy*. Such an ensemble performance is the difficult work/play of engaging in the activity of speaking and creating conversation as transformative of "saying what's on your mind." Here, Vygotsky's challenge to the received wisdom that language expresses thought was essential: "Speech does not merely serve as the expression of developed thought. Thought is restructured as it is transformed into speech. Thought is not expressed but completed in the word" (Vygotsky, 1987, p. 251). We synthesized this instance of Vygotsky's dialectical understanding of human activity with that of Wittgenstein, taking Vygotsky's "speaking completing thinking" as a Wittgensteinian "form of life" (Wittgenstein, 1958, pp. 11, para. 23). We expanded the concept of "completion" to other people; others could "complete" for you. Very young children become speakers of a language with and through others, and we posited that caregivers "complete" babbling babies, and that the babies creatively imitate their completers.

We drew out the implications of this Vygotskian insight throughout the lifespan and concluded that the human ability to create with language—to complete, and be completed by others—can be, for adults as well as for very young children, a continuous process of creating who we are becoming. In terms of therapy, it suggests that speaking about "what's going on for you" is therapeutic because and to the extent that it is a *socially completive activity* and not a transmittal of so-called private states of mind. Thus, the social therapist's task is to support the group in practicing method so as to relate to emotional talk relationally and activistically rather than individualistically and representationally. In this process people experience that they can create and that developing comes with participating in the process of building the groups in which one functions (Holzman, 2009; Holzman & Newman, 2012).

Big Ideas and Revolutionary Activity

The focus of therapy is no longer the individuated self who discovers deeper insights into his or her consciousness. The focus has become the collective that is engaged in the continuous activity of creating a new social unit. The typical therapeutic question, "How is each individual doing?" becomes "How well is the group performing its activity?" This shift from the individual to the group reorganizes what is traditionally related to as a dualistic and antagonistic relationship between individual and group into a dialectical one. Mainstream psychology has tended to negate the group or reduce the group to the individual. Mainstream Marxism has tended to negate the individual or reduce the individual to the group. However, recognizing the "groupness" of human life does not inevitably negate individuals. The social therapy group is producing something collectively and, as with many life activities, individual members contribute in different ways and to differing degrees. Focusing on how the group is performing its activity does not preclude seeing individuals; one can see and relate to both simultaneously.

In terms of Vygotsky's understanding of play, social therapy can be understood as a playful activity in the "head taller" sense. The adult clients are being supported by the therapists to do what is beyond them—to create new ways of speaking and listening to each other, and new ways to understand and relate to talk and to emotionality. By their language play, they are creating new performances of themselves as a way out of the rigidified roles, patterns and identities that cause so much emotional pain.

Areas to Explore (Practical-)Critically

As a practical-critical process ontology, social therapeutic group activity raises some questions that those working to develop critical psychotherapy might wish to explore.

Individual Therapy

What is the purpose of individual therapy? If the unit of study is the group creating itself and the group activity is the tool-and-result practice of reconstructing Marx's species identity/history making, then perhaps the entity experiencing distress (an individual client) need not be the focus of the therapy. Perhaps individuals need to be organized as social units in order to carry out the task of developing. This is, after all, the case for countless other human endeavors in which people become organized as social units to get a specific job done. (Manufacturing, most team sports, theatrical and other performance activities—not to mention the military—come immediately to mind as examples).

Alienation

A second area for exploration is alienation. The alienation that Marx (1974) describes—relating to the products of production severed from their producers and from the process of their production, that is, as commodities—is not limited to smartphones, cars and Big Macs, not even for Marx: "Production does not only produce man as a *commodity*, the *human commodity*, man in the form of a *commodity*; in conformity with this situation it produces him as a *mentally* and *physically dehumanized* being" (Marx, 1967, p. 111). It has become the normal way of seeing and relating to everything in contemporary Western (and, increasingly, global) culture. People relate to their lives, their relationships, their feelings, their culture, and so on, as things, torn away from the process of their creation and from their creators. Such "thingification" is a major factor in people's emotional problems, but rarely spoken about by psychotherapists as something that is engaged in their practices.

However, if, following Marx, we are commodified and alienated individuals, then any transformative social change necessitates de-commodifying and de-alienating such human "products" through a positive and constructive process of producing sociality and regaining humanity. Vygotsky's psychology of being/becoming can be employed (as it has in social therapy) to de-commodify and de-alienate, through a reconstruction-deconstruction of the ontology of modernist psychology in which human beings are understood to be only who we are (hardly world-historic, in Marx's sense). In social therapy's process ontology, human beings are both who we are and who we are becoming. And who we are becoming are creators of tools(-and-results) that can continuously transform mundane specific life practices (including those that produce alienation) into new forms of life. Creating these new kinds of tools is the *becoming activity* of creating/giving expression to our sociality and historicity as revolutionaries.

Power
Finally, we would do well to rethink how we understand and speak of *power*. Critical psychologists and (educators and economists and…) speak of "power" as a pejorative, something bad or even evil, the property of those who rule. Instances of this abound; this book's editors, as one example, speak of "the exercise of power" in the negative. When and how did "power" lose its revolutionary meaning? What happened to "power to the people?" What does it mean to "empower people" if the "exercise of power" is to be avoided? But these are merely different uses of "power" in different contexts, you might be thinking. Yes, they are. And more. To relate to people as revolutionaries (engaged in "all-round development") these multiple meanings need to be deconstructed.

A starting point is to see power in its socio-political sense as distinguished from authority—power being *created from the bottom*, and authority being *imposed from the top*. From this vantage point, being "in power" and "exercising power" are as different as can be. Newman and I drew out the implications of the power/authority dialectic as it is manifest psychologically as we argued that the *activity* of power is practical-critical, revolutionary activity:

> But being "in power" (somewhat ironically) does not at all involve the activity of power. It is, rather, the commodification of power (labor power) into authority. And while commodities can be sold, they do not develop; they are consumed. Authority stifles growth. It is not a neces-

sary evil. It is an unnecessary evil. What is necessary for development is the activity of power, the exercise of power, the development of power by the many—collectively, democratically and creatively. It is the work of the laborer, Marx teaches us, that creates value (Marx, 1967). It is the authoritarian commodification of this process that yields a *realization* of this value which, in turn, maintains the authority of the owners of the means of production.

But authority (vs. power) goes well beyond the economic sphere. It is constantly present, under capitalism, in the psychological sphere. The human capacity to authoritarianly commodify oneself is in constant psychological struggle with the human desire and capacity to exercise power *without commodification*, i.e., freely. (Holzman & Newman, 2004, p. 75)

"Authoritarian commodification" aptly describes professional, institutionalized psychotherapy, counseling and social work in the US and, increasingly, elsewhere. It is epitomized by the nearly universal necessity of a DSM or ICD diagnosis in order to help or be helped. In the face of such dehumanizing by authority, the practical-critical practice of social therapy is one method of supporting people to *exercise power without commodification*. It is this psychological struggle that I urge critical psychotherapy and counseling to support in their work with clients.

References

Friedman, D. (2011). 'Good-bye ideology, hello performance.' *Topoi: An International Review of Philosophy*, 30 (2), 125-35.

Gergen, K. (1991). *The saturated self: Dilemmas of identity in contemporary life*. New York: Basic Books.

Gergen, M. M., & Gergen, K. J. (2012). *Playing with purpose: Adventures in performative social science*. Walnut Creek CA: Left Coast Press.

Holzman, L. (2006). Activating postmodernism. *Theory & Psychology*, 16(1), 109-123.

Holzman, L. (2009). *Vygotsky at work and play*. London and New York: Routledge.

Holzman, L. (2013). Critical psychology, philosophy and social therapy. *Human Studies*, 36, (4,) 471-489. [Chinese translation, 2013, In Bo Wang (Ed.), *Special Issue of Register of Critical Theory of Society: Critical Psychology*. Nanjing: Jiangsu People's Publishing House.]

Holzman L. & Morss, J. R. (Eds.). (2000). *Postmodern psychologies, societal practice, and political life*. New York: Psychology Press.

Holzman, L. & Newman, F. (2012). Activity and performance (and their discourses)in social therapeutic practice. In A. Lock and T. Strong (Eds.), *Discursive perspectives in therapeutic practice* (pp. 184-195). Oxford: Oxford University Press.

Holzman, L. & Newman, F. with Strong, T. (2004). Power, authority and pointless activity: The developmental discourse of social therapy. In T. Strong and D. Paré

(Eds.), *Furthering talk: Advances in discursive therapies* (pp. 73-86). New York: Kluwer Academic.

King, Dr. M. L. Jr. (1056). 27 June 1956 address to the Annual Convention of the NAACP in San Francisco. Retrieved from http://www.mindfreedom.org/kb/mental-health-global/iaacm/MLK-on-IAACM

Kvale, S (1992). *Psychology and postmodernism*. Thousand Oaks, CA: Sage.

Levitin, K. (1982). *One is not born a personality: Profiles of Soviet education psychologists*. Moscow: Progress Publishers.

Lobman, C. & O'Neill, B. (2011) (Eds.). *Play and performance*, Vol. 11, Play & Culture Studies. New York: University Press of America.

Lotringer, S. (1977). Libido unbound: The politics of schizophrenia. *Semiotexte, II*, (3), 7.

Martinez, J. E. (2011). *A performatory approach to teaching, learning and technology*. Rotterdam, The Netherlands: Sense Publishers.

Marx, K. (1967). Economic and philosophical manuscripts. In E. Fromm, *Marx's concept of man* (pp. 90-196). New York: Frederick Ungar Publishing Co.

Marx, K. (1974). Theses on Feuerbach. In K. Marx and F. Engels, *The German Ideology* (pp. 121-3). New York: International Publishers.

Marx, K. & Engels, F. (1974). *The German ideology*. New York: International Publishers.

Newman, F. & Holzman, L. (2014/1993). *Lev Vygotsky: Revolutionary scientist*. London: Routledge.

Newman, F. & Holzman, L. (2006/1996). *Unscientific psychology: A cultural-performatory approach to understanding human life*. Lincoln, NE: iUniverse Inc. (originally published Westport, CT: Praeger).

Newman, F. & Holzman, L. (2003). All power to the developing! *Annual Review of Critical Psychology*, 3, 8-23.

Newman, F. & Holzman, L (1997). *The end of knowing: A new developmental way of learning*. London: Routledge.

Vygotsky, L. S. (1978). *Mind in society*. Cambridge, MA: Harvard University Press.

Vygotsky, L. S. (1987). *The collected works of L. S. Vygotsky, Volume 1*. New York: Plenum.

Wittgenste n L. (1958). *Philosophical investigations*. New York: Macmillan.

Big Ideas and Revolutionary Activity

"Vygotskian-izing" Psychotherapy

"Vygotskyian-izing" Psychotherapy discusses social therapy and its relationship to Lev Vygotsky's sociocultural-historical perspective and his dialectical, activity-based understanding of human development. Drawing from Marx's assertions about the dialectics of human activity and our extraordinary ability to change totalities, Wittgenstein and his conceptions about language games and Vygotsky's own assertions about completion, social therapy assists people in performing new ways of being and doing. Lois shares how bringing these three figures together in dialogue helped her and Newman create a social therapeutic practice that works with groups large and small to perform new versions of themselves, challenging the often damaging "problem-solution" paradigm that produces and perpetuates the debilitating effects of labels/perceptions of self that people bring with them when seeking help.

> *It's sort of taken me out of thinking about what are my problems and what do I need to solve and more about being a part of a group of people that are trying to create something else and do something different.*
>
> *It was a process of unlearning what I thought therapy was about and relearning a new way of living."*
>
> (Responses to the question asked of people in social therapy: "How do you feel being in a therapy that's not about you?")

As a developmental psychologist, contemporary Vygotskian and co-developer of social therapy, the methodology referred to in the comments above, I imagine Vygotsky would be surprised and maybe shocked by what the people said. But I like to think he would be delighted to learn that he inspired a therapeutic approach focused on development through group creativity.

Vygotsky was no Cartesian. He traversed several dualistic divides: biology and culture, behavior and consciousness, thinking and speaking, learning and development, and individual and social. Refusing to accept the foundational dualism of psychological conceptualization and arguing forcefully (although sometimes conflictedly and less than thoroughly) against it, he urged instead a method of dialectics. His writings on these matters have been the foundation of much contemporary research. Far less recognized but equally important is Vygotsky's challenge to psychology's dualistic conceptualization of cognition and emotion: "Among the most basic defects of traditional approaches to the study of psychology has been the isolation of the intellectual from the volitional and affective aspects of consciousness" (1987, p. 50).[1]

Perhaps as a consequence of overlooking Vygotsky's position that "there exists a

Big Ideas and Revolutionary Activity

dynamic meaningful system that constitutes *a unity of affective and intellectual processes*" (Vygotsky, 1987, p. 50), the great majority of psychologists and educational researchers influenced by Vygotsky continue to isolate one from the other and perpetuate "a one-sided view of the human personality" (Vygotsky, 1983, vol.3, p. 57, quoted in Gajdamaschko, 2005, p. 14). The result is that while Vygotsky's ideas have been studied in relation to dozens of intellectual disciplines and areas of professional practice, psychotherapy, emotions and emotional development have yet to be "Vygotskian-ized." With few exceptions, contemporary Vygotskians have stayed clear of these areas, and the majority of psychotherapy researchers and clinical practitioners have little familiarity with Vygotsky. [2]

The lack of attention to Vygotsky's work by clinical psychology and psychotherapy is unfortunate, and becomes more troublesome as these areas of research and practice are forced by regulatory and licensing bodies, psychiatry, and insurance companies to move farther and farther away from social-cultural understandings and practices. As someone who has been "Vygotskian-izing" psychotherapy for over thirty years, I have gained some understanding of the paradigmatic constraints and biases of psychology that can account for both the difficulty in recognizing and acting upon Vygotsky's insistence that cognition and emotion are a dialectical unity, and for the lack of Vygotskian thinking applied to psychotherapy.

Since its creation thirty-five years ago by philosopher Fred Newman, social therapy has been greatly influenced by what Newman and I take to be Vygotsky's revolutionary methodology, which we and others have made use of in developing a therapeutic and, more broadly, human development practice (Holzman, 2009; Holzman & Mendez, 2003; Newman & Holzman, 1993). I have a particular framework for understanding the depth and breadth of psychology's cognitive bias. In no small part, the decades of practicing, teaching and articulating social therapeutics has been the activity of breaking with the cognitive-emotive divide. This engagement and the combination of enthusiasm and skepticism toward the endeavor have helped me appreciate the depth of the cognitive bias.

Emotion and Psychotherapy

Western culture has not been kind to emotion. It's been ignored, demeaned and outcast as inferior to cognition, the enemy of rationality, characteristically female (and, thereby, unworthy of attention) for centuries. Certainly, feminist psychologists and philosophers have made significant contributions in exposing the male biases of accepted conceptions of being human since the 1960s, but the overall cultural environment of psychology, both theoretically and institutionally, remains paradigmatically male and cognitively overdetermined. Psychotherapy, the area of psychology most identified with emotion, is generally thought of as soft science, or not science at all. This assessment is applauded by those who relate to psychotherapy as an art or cultural activity, and lamented by those who work to advance its scientific credentials. The last two decades have seen the profession bowing to pressure or taking up the mantle (depending on one's point of view) to become more "scientific" (objective, measurable, "evidence-based," etc.), even as female psychotherapists outnumber their male counterparts, a trend also noted for psychology as a whole (American Psychologist, 2006 and http://www.apa.org/gradpsych/2011/01/cover-men.aspx). A welcome innovation occurring in the profession is the shift to relationality (which makes use of the feminist conception of connection, for example, Miller, 1976). But in the overall conservative environment in which this shift is taking place relationality is not only marginalized but highly vulnerable to being cast in cognitive terms.

A striking measure of the cognitive bias is in the field of psychotherapy itself, in which the dominant way of relating to emotional pain, for the past two decades or so, has been with cognitive and behavioral therapies. Apparently, emotions have all but disappeared in this process. How absent emotions have been from psychotherapy training and literature is evidenced by recent books, articles and conferences that frame clients' emotional lives as a new frontier in psychotherapy and offer therapists opportunities to learn how to make use of emotions in their therapeutic encounters. For example, the 2011 American Academy of Psychotherapists conference, "The Role of Emotion in Psychotherapy," had the following rationale: "...because of recent trends in academic psychology and research based training programs, emotional processes and the need for expressive/experiential affective interventions have been undervalued or eschewed as important clinical skills. Hence the need to reinforce the value of the role of emotions in psychotherapy" (http://www.aapweb.com/files/SouthernRegion_Brochure_4-11.pdf).

More telling is the popular online resource for therapists, the *Psychotherapy Networker*, which has been promoting their series, "The Power of Emotions," as a way for practitioners to "Gain the understanding, insight, and know-how to engage authentically with clients as emotions emerge [because] working with emotions can be tough for both clients and therapists. This series is designed both to deepen your understanding of emotions and to strengthen your ability to work with them effectively" (http://www.psychotherapynetworker.org/cecourses/networker-plugged-in/emotion-web-series).

At least in part, the surge of interest in emotion is coming from discoveries in neuroscience—which, even from reading only the popular press, seem to be made each day (and which are fascinating). But what are others doing with these discoveries? Quoting the *Psychotherapy Networker* again, "Neuroscientists have recently established that emotion is the prime organizing force shaping how we cope with challenges...emotion is anything but primitive and unpredictable. It's a complex, exquisitely efficient information-processing system, designed to organize behavior rapidly in the interests of survival" (http://www.psychotherapynetworker.org/magazine/recentissues/2012-mayjune/item/1702-the-power-of-emotion-in-therapy).

This sounds just like a typical description of cognition, doesn't it? Apparently, in order to bring emotionality to the attention of therapists, it has to be framed in cognitive terms and, thereby, legitimized.

This is but the most recent manifestation of the cognitive bias and natural science view of emotion that has shaped psychotherapy and clinical psychology. At the same time, social-cultural alternatives to overly cognitive therapies have been created. Among them is social therapy, an approach directly influenced by Vygotsky's work, to which I now turn.

Vygotsky's Tool-and-Result Method and Social Therapy

Social therapy originated in the 1970s as part of the social-cultural change movements of the time, which tied the "personal" to the political. Similar to other new psychologies springing up at the time, it was ideology-based: its reason for being was that living under capitalism makes people emotionally sick and the hope was that therapy could be a tool in the service of progressive politics. Like the radical therapies of the 1970s, social therapy engaged the authoritarianism, sexism, racism, classism and homophobia of traditional psychotherapy. But social therapy's unique feature was its engagement of the philosophical underpinnings of psychology and psychotherapy; it rejected explanation, interpretation, the notion of an inner self that therapists and clients need to delve into, and other dualistic and problematic foundations of traditional psychology—a characteristic of what are now known as postmodern psychologies (e.g., Fee, 2000; Frie, 2003; Gergen, 1991; Holzman & Morss, 2000; Kvale, 1992). As an emerging practical-critical epistemological and ontological critique, social therapy was influenced by Newman's study of Marxian dialectics and the philosophy of science and language (Wittgenstein's work in particular), and my study of human development and Vygotsky and work as a neo-Vygotskian researcher. Marx, Vygotsky and Wittgenstein—their methodological innovations in particular—helped us see the potential for ordinary people to effect radical social change and better understand the subjective constraints that need to be engaged so as to actualize this potential (e.g., Holzman, 2006; Newman & Holzman, 2006/1996; 2003). The current discussion will touch upon all three but focus on Vygotsky.

The relevance of Vygotsky to psychotherapy, instantiated in social therapy, is centered on his dialectical method. Vygotsky was an important figure in the debates in the early 20th century over the direction psychology would take. It was on its way to becoming an empirical and experimental science and questions of method and units of analysis were hotly debated. Would following an experimental path mean that the very nature of human consciousness would be excluded from psychological investigation? Vygotsky was not willing to give up the study of consciousness. Nor would he settle for two kinds of psychology (a subjective one for mental events and an objective one for non-mental events) or for one psychology that reduced mental events to non-mental ones, thus bypassing consciousness. These option, he argued, rested on an erroneous belief in an objectivist epistemology, which, in effect, denies science as a human (meaning-making) activity and mistakenly treats human beings as natural phenomena. For Vygotsky, psychology as a human science could not develop so long as it was based in objective-subjective dualism. The method of natural science might work for studying natural phenomena, but not for the study of human beings. A psychology with a natural science method contains "an insoluble methodological contradiction. It is a natural science about unnatural things" and produces "a system of knowledge which is contrary to them" (Vygotsky, 2004, p. 298). A scientific study of human beings required a nondualistic method, a precondition of which was a nondualistic *conception of method*:

> The search for method becomes one of the most important problems of the entire enterprise of understanding the uniquely human forms of psychological activity. In this case, the method is simultaneously prerequisite and product, the tool and the result of the study. (Vygotsky, 1978, p. 65)

Vygotsky was proposing a radical break with the accepted scientific paradigm in which method is a tool that is applied and yields results. In this case, the relation between tool and result is linear, instrumental and dualistic, what Newman and I call *tool-for-result methodology* (Newman & Holzman, 1993). Vygotsky proposed a different conception of method—not a tool to be applied, but an activity (a "search") that generates both tool and result at the same time and as continuous process. Tool and result are not dualistically separated, neither are they the same or one thing. Rather, they are elements of a dialectical unity/totality/whole. Method to be practiced, not applied, is what Vygotsky was advocating. To capture the dialectical relationship of this new conception, Newman and I call this *tool-and-result methodology* (Newman & Holzman, 1993). This new conception of method is neither objective nor subjective, but something outside that dualistic box.

In making this break with the psychology of his time, Vygotsky brought Marx's insights to bear on the practical question of how human beings learn and develop.[3] The unique feature of human individual, cultural and species development is human activity, which is qualitative and transformative (unlike behavior change, which is particularistic and cumulative). Human beings do not merely respond to stimuli, acquire societally determined and useful skills, and adapt to the determining environment. The uniqueness of human social life is that we ourselves transform the determining circumstances. Human development is not an individual accomplishment but a *socio-cultural activity*.

The distinction between tool-and-result and tool-for-result is relevant to how people of any culture see and relate to themselves and the people and stuff of the world. In the west, we have been socialized to see through the lens of the problem-solution paradigm. Problems are the "stuff" of life in the western (ized) world, and with problems come solutions, even if not always realized. People see and understand themselves and others in terms and language of problems. We are taught to see problems and to search for solutions. Doing "good" science (diplomacy, education, government, etc). has come to mean correctly identifying the problems and coming up with solutions to them. Despite the failure of this mode of seeing and thinking

Big Ideas and Revolutionary Activity

in the human development realm (for example, raising children, living peacefully or eliminating poverty), the problem-solution paradigm dominates, severely constraining people's capacity to envision possibilities of transforming the world.

The problem-solution paradigm is foundational to how psychotherapy has come to be understood and practiced. It is a field dominated by the problematizing of emotional life. Going to a therapist means that something is wrong, and the therapist's first task is to identify the "presenting problem." For the mainstream psychotherapist, the work is finding the solution to the problem, first by naming it and then by going through (sometimes with the client, sometimes not) a process of discovering the cause or source of the problem, by prescribing medication, or by some combination of the two. Institutionalized psychotherapy is so organized around problems that if you do not have one that is identifiable according to the *Diagnostic and Statistical Manual of Mental Disorders*, you can be denied treatment (e.g., Ednos—"eating disorder not otherwise specified," Henig, 2004).

The *DSM-5*, the 2013 revision of the manual, was a source of great controversy and much publicity in 2011-12. While much of the outcry had to do with the pseudo-scientific way the manual was generated, an equal amount came from parents and service providers concerned that changes in diagnostic categories would lessen needed services. Among the most controversial was the elimination of Asperger's syndrome as a distinct disorder and its incorporation into the autism spectrum disorder—the fear being that there would no longer be a category of mental illness to draw on for reimbursement (e.g., Compart, 2012; Lutz, 2013).

More broadly, there has been decades-long criticism of diagnosis as a requirement for psychotherapy, including pleas to abandon the medical model and view psychotherapy as an art and not a science. However, there is less critical discussion of the problem-solution paradigm that underlies it. Pointing out that the person is not the problem, but "has" a problem for example, does not deny the problem-solution paradigm. Again, the cognitive bias is at play, for the problem-solution paradigm is, at base, a cognitive model of emotionality.

The methodology with which to tackle a world filled with problems is an instrumental one. Tool-for-result methodology is the epistemological counterpart to the ontology of problems and solution. It is essentially a problem-solving approach. In contrast, tool-and-result methodology rejects this way of viewing and living in the world, in favor of a more unified, emergent and continuous process approach. The goal of psychotherapy of the tool-and-result variety is to support people to create, not to problem solve.

Psychotherapies of this type are collaborative, with therapists and clients together creating the therapy. They are exercises in meaning making. Above all, they are relational, not only in focusing on the co-creative relationship of therapists and clients, but also as seeing and relating to emotion as relational.[4] The creative work in social therapy involves producing new emotionality inseparable from new ways of relating to emotionality.

From this dialectical tool-and-result conception of method of Vygotsky stem three important insights.

Learning and Development
Vygotsky's view of how development and learning are related remains unconventional. Rejecting the view that learning depends on and follows development, Vygotsky conceptualized learning and development as a dialectical unity in which learning is ahead of or leads development: "Instruction is only useful when it moves ahead of development. When it does, it impels or wakens a whole series of functions that are in a stage or maturation lying in the zone of proximal development" (1987, p. 212). Newman and I came to understand "learning-leading-development" (or "learning-and-development"— both being shorthands for Vygotsky's conception) as an important advance in bringing Marx's dialectical conception of activity to psychology (Newman & Holzman, 1993). To us, Vygotsky was not saying that learning literally comes first, or that it leads development in a linear or temporal fashion. He was saying that as social-cultural, relational activities, learning and development are inseparable; they are a unity in which learning is connected to and leads —dialectically, not linearly—development. Learning and development co-generate each other. Attention must be paid to understanding the kinds of environments that create and support this co-generation, and how such environments differ from those that do not—including environments that divorce development from learning and have acquisitional learning as their goal, i.e., most schools (Holzman, 1997).

Such a developmental environment is apparent in Vygotsky's descriptions of how very young children become speakers of a language, where babies and their caretakers are engaged in the tool-and-result activity of creating the environment and the learning-and-development at the same time through their language play. This is a picture of what the dialectical process of being/becoming looks like—very young children are related to simultaneously as who they are (babies who babble) and who they are not/who they are becoming (speakers), and that this is how they develop as speakers/learn language.

In developmental learning environments such as this, Vygotsky showed that children learn collectively and through their active relationships with others at varying levels of skill, knowledge, expertise, ability and personality. They are not yet socialized to the cultural norm that one *must know*. They have not yet evolved the "epistemic posture" (Holzman, 2009). They learn by doing with others what they do not know how to do because the group (usually the family) supports such active, creative risk taking. This view of developmental learning is applicable to "therapeutic" learning. People in therapy learn to do "therapy talk" through being supported by the therapist to do so, not because they knew how to do it before they walked into the therapist's office. Group therapy maximizes the potential growth because clients must build active relationships with others at varying levels of skill, knowledge, expertise, ability and personality.

Play

Next is Vygotsky's understanding of the role of play in child development. Vygotsky distinguished between play and learning in the developmental process, but there are important similarities between them nevertheless. Of special significance is the following: "In play a child always behaves beyond his average age, above his daily behavior; in play it is as though he were a head taller than himself" (Vygotsky, 1978, p. 102). Newman and I took "a head taller" as a metaphor for the being/becoming dialectic of human development-and-learning, the activity of "being who you are" and "who you are becoming/other than who you are" simultaneously. Aside from young children, the other grouping of people who are supported to be simultaneously who they are and other (than who they are) are actors on the stage. Theatrical performance and children's play share this dialectical quality. Performance, we suggest, is a form of Vygotskian play through which human beings collectively perform their development. For most adults, the non-knowing, imaginative activity of play and the support for "performing a head taller" dissipate beyond childhood. In order for people to continue to develop (and learn developmentally) they need to relearn how to play as children do but in ways that are appropriate to being adults. They need support to perform a head taller. We began to see social therapy groups as the activity of seeing and relating to people as performers of their affective-cognitive lives.

Vygotsky's zone of proximal development (zpd) is critical to the notion that performing is how human beings create development. The zpd appears at different times and in multiple translations of Vygotsky's writings, and in relation to both learning and play, yielding varying understandings of the zpd among contemporary Vygotskians.[5]

The characterization most relevant to a Vygotskian-izing of psychotherapy is that which emphasizes the social collectivity of the zpd. For example, in "The Collective as a Factor in the Development of the Abnormal Child," Vygotsky characterized the social level of development as "a function of collective behavior, as a form of cooperation or cooperative activity" (Vygotsky, 2004, p. 202). Linking this with Vygotsky's tool-and-result method, the zpd becomes a collective activity whereby the creating of the "zone" simultaneously produces the learning-and-development of the collective. Thus, the zpd is process rather than spatio-temporal entity, and activity rather than place, space or distance. It is dialectical, tool-and-result activity, simultaneously the creating of the zone (environment) and what is created (learning-and-development). Further, the zpd highlights the dialectic of human life (being/becoming). Creating the zpd involves relating to people as capable of doing what they do not yet know how to do and what is, therefore, beyond them—what Vygotsky described as "the child's potential to move from what he is able to do to what he is not,"

(Vygotsky, 1987, p. 212). As applied to social therapy groups, groupings of people collectively work together and create the "zone of emotional development" that *is* their new emotionality (their learning-and-development). As in the zpd of childhood described by Vygotsky, people at different levels of experience and skill employ a creative methodology of producing environments in which and how they organize and reorganize their relationships to themselves, each other and to the tools (both material and psychological) and objects of their world. They construct "zones" that allow them *to become*.

Completion

Vygotsky also challenged the received wisdom about thought and language, offering an alternative to the expressionist, representational and correspondence views of language. Speaking, he said, is not the outward expression of thinking, but part of a unified, transformative process. "Speech does not merely serve as the expression of developed thought. Thought is restructured as it transformed into speech. Thought is not expressed but completed in the word" (Vygotsky, 1987, p. 251). And, "The relationship of thought to word is not a thing but a process, a movement from thought to word and from word to thought. Thought is not expressed but completed in the word. Any thought has movement. It unfolds" (Vygotsky, 1987, p. 250).

With language and thought as dialectical process and unified activity, the psychological divide between inner and outer disappear. There are no longer two separate worlds, the private one of thinking and the social one of speaking. There is, instead, the complex dialectical unity, speaking/thinking, in which speaking completes thinking. If speaking is the completing of thinking, as Vygotsky says, if the process is continuously creative in socio-cultural space, then it follows that the "completer" does not have to be the one who is doing the thinking. Others can complete for us. And when they do, they are no more saying what we are thinking than we are saying what we are thinking when we complete ourselves. Looping back to how very young children become speakers of a language with and through others, Newman and I posited that caretakers 'complete" babbling babies, and that the babies creatively imitate their completers. We drew out the implications of this Vygotskian insight for how to create learning-and-development opportunities throughout the life span, including the therapy office. In psychotherapy, whatever the modality, talking about one's inner life is therapeutic because and to the extent that it is a socially completive activity and not a transmittal of private states of mind. The human ability to create with language—to complete, and be completed by, others—is a continuous process of creating who we are becoming, a tool-and-result of the activity of developing (Holzman, 2009).

Understanding language as a socially completive activity raises questions about "the truth" of people's words and, by extension, the concept of truth itself. One can reject an expressionist view of language and with it the notion of objective truth. For those psychologists and psychotherapists who do so, talk therapy is not done in order to discover some hidden truth of someone's life, to find the true cause of emotional pain or to apply the one true method of treatment, because truth in that form (Truth) does not exist. Instead, they construct subjective theories of truth and devise practices consistent with them. For example, social constructionists search for relational forms of dialogue as an alternative to objectivist-based debate and criticism; narrative therapists work to expose the "storiness" of our lives and help people create their own (and, most often, better) stories; and collaborative therapists emphasize the dynamic and co-constructed nature of meaning.

However, from the social-therapeutic point of view, to posit truth as subjective, with the existence of multiple truths (all with a small "t"), does not escape objective-subjective dualism. Truth may be socially constructed in these approaches, but dualism remains intact, as there must be something about which it can be said, "It is true (or false)." In contrast, relating to therapeutic talk as socially completive activity in Vygotsky's sense is a rejection of truth and its opposite, falsity. The social therapeutic shift to activity is a way to transform therapeutic talk from being an appeal to or about both objective, outer reality Truth and subjective, inner cognitive or emotive truths. As socially completive activity, therapy talk is a consciously self-reflexive engagement of the creating of the talk itself. In performing therapy, the fictional nature of "the truth" of our everyday language, our everyday psychology and our everyday stories gets exposed as people have the opportunity to experience themselves as the collective creators of their emotional activity. It is, in Wittgenstein's words, the playing language games and a form of life.[6]

Creative Imitation

According to Vygotsky, "A full understanding of the concept of the zone of proximal development must result in a reevaluation of the role of imitation in learning" (1978, p. 87). He discounted the mechanical view of imitation that was "rooted in traditional psychology, as well as in everyday consciousness" and the individualistically biased inferences drawn from it, for example, that "the child can imitate anything" and that "what I can do by imitating says nothing about my own mind" (1987, p. 209). To him, imitation was an active, creative and fundamentally social process that was essential to creating the zpd. Children do not imitate anything and everything as a parrot does, but rather what is beyond them in their environment/relationships. *Creatively imitating* others in their daily interactions —saying what someone else says, moving to music, picking up a pencil and "writing"—is relating to oneself as/being related to by others as/performing as a speaker, a dancer, a writer, a learner, a human being. It is how children are capable of doing so much in collective activity.

Vygotsky's analysis of the language-learning zpd in *Thinking and Speech* is an excellent illustration of creative imitation at work. He showed that babies and toddlers do not learn language nor are they taught language in the cognitive, acquisitional and transmittal sense typical of institutionalized learning and teaching. They develop as speakers, language makers and language users as an inseparable part of joining and transforming the social life of their family (community, group). When babies begin to babble they are speaking before they know how by virtue of the speakers around them creating conversation with them. Mothers, fathers, grandparents, siblings and others neither tell babies that they are too young, correct them, give them a grammar book and dictionary to study, nor remain silent around them. Rather, they relate to infants and babies as capable of far more than they could possibly do "naturally." They relate to them as fellow speakers, feelers, thinkers and makers of meaning. This is what makes it possible for very young children to do what they are not yet capable of. The babbling baby's rudimentary speech is a *creative imitation* of the more developed speaker's speech. At the same time, the more developed speakers "complete" the baby, and the "conversation" continues.

Creative imitation is a type of performance. When they are playing with language in this way in the language-learning zpd, babies are simultaneously performing—*becoming*—themselves. Performing is a way of taking "who we are" and creating something new through incorporating "the other"—on the stage a newly emerging character and in this case a newly emerging speaker.

While linking creative imitation with performance, and performance with the dialectic being/becoming that is development, may seem at first glance to be far from Vygotsky's work, its roots are there in his writings. Particularly relevant is an essay published in English in Volume 4 of his collected works ("Conclusion; Further Research; Development of Personality and World View in the Child," Vygotsky, 1997). Linking early childhood play to the formation of personality and worldview, Vygotsky wrote that the preschool child "can be somebody else just as easily as he can be himself" (p. 249). Vygotsky attributed this to the child's lack of recognition that s/he is an "I" and went on to discuss how personality and play transform through later childhood.

Vygotsky did not make note of a downside to the transformations in the young child's performance ability. As children perform their way into cultural and societal adaptation, their potential for continuous development becomes limited. What they have learned through performing becomes routinized and rigidified. By middle school, many children have become so skilled at acting out certain roles that they no longer keep creating new performances of themselves (that is, developing). By the time they are adults, most people have an identity as "this kind of person"—someone who does certain things (and does them in certain ways) and feels certain ways. Anything other than that would not be "true" to "who *I* am." This is the identity that people bring into therapy.

Building upon Vygotsky's observation about young children's performance ability, performing as someone else (being oneself and other than oneself) can be seen as the source of development. For Vygotsky, this is at the time of life before "I" and its culturally produced fixed identity. For social therapists, it can be throughout the life course. Social therapeutic methodology has evolved into a conscious effort to revitalize this human capacity.

Big Ideas and Revolutionary Activity

Zones of Emotional Development

The primary modality of social therapy is group because its potential to challenge particularism and individualism is greater than "individual" (one-on-one) psychotherapy.

In social therapy, the group is the therapeutic unit. This distinguishes social therapy from most group therapies, in which the group is not itself the therapeutic unit but, rather, serves as a context for the therapist to help individuals with their emotional problems. Clients who come together to form a social therapy group are given the task to create their group as an environment in which they can get help. This group activity is a collective, practical challenge to the assumption that the way people get therapeutic help is to relate to themselves and be related to by others as individuals, complete with problems and with inner selves.

Social therapy groups conducted in centers for social therapy in the US are comprised of 10-25 people, a mix of women and men of varying ages, ethnicities, sexual orientations, class backgrounds and economic status, professions and "presenting problems." The groups are consciously heterogeneous for two reasons: 1) to challenge people's notion of a fixed identity (e.g., based on gender, ethnicity, diagnostic label, or "That's the kind of person I am"); and 2) the more diverse the elements, the more material there is with which to create. Groups are typically ongoing and meet weekly for 90 minutes. Some group members remain for years, others months; people leave and new members join. The elements of the therapeutic zpd are thus continuously changing. (In other countries social therapy is practiced in a structure and manner that is coherent with the specifics of the given cultural environments and differs accordingly from this description).

People come to social therapy, as they do to any therapy or any group setting, individuated. They say things like, "My daughter and I were screaming at each other last night. I was so angry at her and now I feel awful;" "I couldn't get out of bed this week;" "I don't know how to talk to my father since he got so sick;" "I feel really crazy, like I'm not here, and it scares me." They look to the therapist for some advice, solution, interpretation, or explanation. They want to feel better and have more control over their lives.

The members of social therapy groups come together and participate in creating their group. The social therapist works with the group (not with the individuated selves that comprise the group) to organize itself as an *emotional zpd*. Members of the group raise whatever they want and however they want, which is typically how they're feeling, an emotional problem, a relationship going bad, or something upsetting that happened to them. This is the material out of which to create; the members, each at different levels of emotional development, are encouraged, invited, supported and challenged to create *the group's* level of emotional development. The group has to figure out how to talk about what they want to talk about. In western cultures people relate to feelings as individuated and private, a factor that contributes to feeling isolated and alone with the "possession" of their feelings. Creating the social therapy group entails creating a relational understanding and language of emotionality. The group's task is to babble, play with language, creatively imitate and complete each other and the therapist, and make meaning together. Speaking as truth telling, reality representing, inner thought and feeling revealing—these deeply held (if typically not in conscious awareness) beliefs about the functions of language are challenged as people falteringly attempt to converse in new ways, to create something new out of their initial individuated, problem-oriented presentations of self.

Talking about one's inner life is therapeutic because and to the extent that it is a socially completive activity and not a transmittal of private states of mind. The human ability to create with language—to complete, and be completed by, others—can be, for adults as well as for very young children, a continuous process of creating who we are becoming.

The social therapist's task is to lead the group in this activity of discovering a method of relating to emotional talk relationally rather than individualistically, and as activistic rather than as representational. In this process people can come to appreciate what—and that—they can create, and simultaneously to realize the limitations of trying to learn, grow and create individually. If and as the group gradually comes to understand this, different members at different moments realize that growth comes from participating in the process of building the groups in which one functions. This new learning, in a Vygotskian, zpd-like fashion, rekindles development by virtue of the group growing. Traditional therapy's focus on the individuated self who discovers deeper insights into his or her consciousness is transformed into the collective engaged in the continuous activity of creating a new social unit, the emotional zpd. The therapeutic question transforms from "How is each individual doing?" to "How well is the group performing its activity?"

Such a shift in focus from the individual to the group reorganizes what is traditionally related to as a dualistic and antagonistic relationship between individual and group into a dialectical one. Mainstream psychology has tended to negate the group or reduce the group to the individual. Mainstream Marxism has tended to negate the individual or reduce the individual to the group. This need not be the case. Recognizing the groupness of human life does not inevitably negate individuals. The group is engaged in producing something collectively and, as with many life activities, individual members contribute in different ways and to differing degrees.

The activity of creating the emotional zpd can be seen as a re-learning of how to learn developmentally, that is, learning collectively, playfully and non-cognitively overdetermined. Vygotsky's accounting of how children develop as speakers of a language seemed a reasonable fit with what transpires in social therapy in the sense that the adult clients are being supported by the therapists to do what is beyond them--to create new ways of speaking and listening to each other, and new ways to understand and relate to talk and to emotionality. By their language play, they are creating new performances of themselves as a way out of the rigidified roles, patterns and identities that cause so much emotional pain.

Big Ideas and Revolutionary Activity

As a Vygotskian-izing of psychotherapy, social therapy plays (perhaps, some would say, loosely) with Vygotsky's search for method. The dialectic of tool-and-result flows through its practice of relating to people as performers of their lives who have the capacity to create a new collective form of working/playing together. It is an attempt to ameliorate the painful and destructive impact that psychology's cognitive-emotive divide has on people's everyday lives.

References

Anderson, H. (1997). *Conversation, language and possibilities: A postmodern approach to therapy*. New York: Basic Books.

Anderson, H. & Gehart, D. (2007). (Eds.), *Collaborative therapy: Relationships and conversations that make a difference*. New York: Routledge.

Baker, G. P. (1992). Some remarks on "language" and "grammar." *Grazer Philosophische Studien, 42,* 107-131.

Cole, M. & Scribner, S. (1974). *Culture and thought: A psychological introduction.* New York: John Wiley.

Compart, P. (2012). Updates to the APA in *DSM-V*—What do the changes mean to families living with autism? Retrieved from http://www.autism.com/index.php/news_dsmV

Fee, D. (Ed.). (2000). *Pathology and the postmodern: Mental illness as discourse and experience.* New York: Sage Publications Limited.

Frie, R. (2003). *Understanding experience: Psychotherapy and postmodernism.* London: Routledge.

Gajdamaschko, N. (2005). Vygotsky on imagination: Why an understanding of the imagination is an important issue for schoolteachers. *Teaching Education, 16,(1),* 13-22.

Gergen, K. (1992). *The saturated self: Dilemmas of identity in contemporary life.* New York: Basic Books.

Gergen, K. J. (2009). *Relational being: Beyond self and community.* Oxford and New York: Oxford University Press.

Gergen, M. M., & Gergen, K. J. (2012). *Playing with purpose: Adventures in performative social science.* Walnut Creek, CA: Left Coast Press.

Glick J. (2004). The history of the development of higher mental function. In R.W. Rieber and D. K. Robinson (Eds.), *The essential Vygotsky.* New York: Kluwer Academic/Plenum Publishers.

González Rey, F. (1999). The subjective character of human activity. In. S. Chaiklin, M. Hedegaard & J. Jensen (Eds.), *Activity theory and social practice* [pp. 253-275]. Aaurhus, Denmark: Aarhus University Press.

González Rey, F. (2007). Social and individual subjectivity from an historical cultural standpoint. *Critical Social Studies. Outlines, 9*(2), 3 -14.

Henig, R.M. (2004). Sorry. Your eating disorder doesn't meet our criteria. *New York*

Times, November 30, 2004.

Holzman, L. (1997). *Schools for growth: Radical alternatives to current educational models.* Mahwah, NJ: Erlbaum.

Holzman, L. (1999). (Ed.), *Performing psychology: A postmodern culture of the mind.* New York: Routledge.

Holzman, L. (2006). Activating postmodernism. *Theory & Psychology, 16*(1), 109-123.

Holzman, L. & Mendez, R. (2003). *Psychological investigations: A clinician's guide to social therapy.* New York: Brunner-Routledge.

Holzman, L. & Morss, J. (Eds). (2000). *Postmodern psychologies, societal practice and political life.* New York: Routledge.

Kvale, S. (Ed.). (1992). *Psychology and postmodernism* (Vol. 9). Thousand Oaks, CA: Sage Publications Limited.

Lock, A. & Strong, T. (2010). *Social constructionism: Sources and stirrings in theory and practice.* Cambridge: Cambridge University Press.

Lutz, A. (2013). You do not have Asperger's—What psychiatry's new diagnostic manual means for people on the autism spectrum. Retrieved from http://www.slate.com/articles/health_and_science/medical_examiner/2013/05/autism_spectrum_diagnoses_the_dsm_5_eliminates_asperger_s_and_pdd_nos.html

Marx, K. (1967). Economic and philosophical manuscripts. In E. Fromm, *Marx's concept of man* (pp. 90-196). New York: Frederick Ungar Publishing Co.

Marx, K. (1974). Theses on Feuerbach. In K. Marx & F. Engels, *The German Ideology* (pp. 121-3). New York: International Publishers.

Marx, K. & Engels, F. (1974). *The German ideology.* New York: International Publishers.

McLeod, J. (1997). *Narrative and psychotherapy.* London: Sage.

McNamee, S. & Gergen, K. J. (Eds.), (1992). *Therapy as social construction.* London: Sage.

McNamee, S. & Gergen, K. J. and Associates (1999). *Relational responsibility: Resources for sustainable dialogue.* Thousand Oaks, CA: Sage.

Miller, J. B. (1976). *Toward a new psychology of women.* Boston: Beacon.

Monk, R. (1990). *Ludwig Wittgenstein: The duty of genius.* NY: Penguin.

Monk, G., Winslade, J., Crocket, K. & Epston, D. (Eds). (1997). *Narrative therapy in practice: The archaeology of hope.* San Francisco: Jossey-Bass.

Newman, F. & Holzman, L. (1993). *Lev Vygotsky: Revolutionary scientist.* London: Routledge.

Newman, F. & Holzman, L. (1997). *The end of knowing: A new developmental way of learning.* London: Routledge.

Newman, F. & Holzman, L. (2006/1996). *Unscientific psychology: A cultural-performatory approach to understanding human life.* Lincoln, NE: iUniverse Inc. (originally published Westport, CT: Praeger).

Paré, D.A. & Larner, G. (2004). (Eds.), *Collaborative practice in psychology and therapy*. NY: Haworth Clinical Practice Press.

Rosen, H. & Kuehlwein, K. T. (Eds). (1996). *Constructing realities: Meaning-making perspectives for psychotherapists*. San Francisco: Jossey-Bass.

Sampson, E. E. (1993). *Celebrating the other*. Hemelhempstead, UK: Harvester Wheatsheaf.

Seikkula, J. (1993). The aim of therapy is to generate dialogue: Bakhtin and Vygotsky in family session. *Human Systems, 3*, 33-48.

Seikkula, J. (2003). Dialogue is the change: Understanding psychotherapy as a semiotic process of Bakhtin, Voloshinov, and Vygotsky. *Human Systems: The Journal of Systemic Consultation & Management, 14 (2)*, 83-94.

Shotter, J. (1989). Vygotsky's psychology: Joint activity in the zone of proximal development. *New Ideas in Psyhcology, 7*, 185-204.

Shotter, J. (1993). *Cultural politics of everyday life: Social constructionism, rhetoric and knowing of the third kind*. Toronto: University of Toronto Press.

Shotter, J. (2000). Seeing historically: Goethe and Vygotsky's 'enabling theory-method'. *Culture and Psychology, 6 (2)*, 233-252.

Shotter, J. (2006). Vygotsky and consciousness as *conscientia*, as witnessable knowing along with other. *Theory & Psychology, 16 (1)*, 13-36.

Smagorinsky, P. (2011). Confessions of a mad professor: An autoethnographic consideration of neuroatypicality, extranormativity, and education. *Teachers College Record*, 113(8), 1701-1732.

Smagorinsky, P. (2012). "Every individual has his own insanity": Applying Vygotsky's work on defectology to the question of mental health as an issue of inclusion. *Learning, Culture and Social Interaction 1*, 67–77.

Soyland, A. J, (1994). *Psychology as metaphor*. London: Sage.

Strong, T. & Lock, A. (Eds.). (2012). *Discursive perspectives in therapeutic practices*. London: Oxford University Press.

Strong, T. & Paré, D.A. (2004). (Eds.), *Furthering talk: Advances in discursive therapies*. New York: Kluwer Academic.

van der Merwe, W. L. & Voestermans, P. P. (1995). Wittgenstein's legacy and the challenge to psychology. *Theory & psychology, 5*(1), 27-48.

Vygotsky, L.S. (1978). *Mind in society*. Cambridge, MA: Harvard University Press.

Vygotsky, L. S. (1987). *The collected works of L. S. Vygotsky. Vol. 1*. New York: Plenum.

Vygotsky, L.S. (1993). *The collected works of L.S. Vygotsky, Volume 2, The fundamentals of defectology*. NY: Plenum.

Vygotsky, L.S. (1994). The problem of the environment. In R. van der Veer & J. Valsiner (Eds.), *The Vygotsky reader* (pp. 338-354). Oxford: Blackwell.

Vygotsky, L.S. (1997). The historical meaning of the crisis in psychology: A methodological investigation. In *The collected works of L.S.Vygotsky, Volume 3* (pp. 233-343). NY: Plenum.

Vygotsky, L.S. (2004). The collective as a factor in the development of the abnormal child. In R.W. Rieber and D. K. Robinson (Eds.), *The essential Vygotsky* (pp. 201-219). NY: Kluwer Academic/Plenum Publishers.

White, M. (2006). *Maps of narrative practice*. NY: W.W. Norton.

White, M. & Epston, D. (1990). *Narrative means to therapeutic ends*. New York: W.W. Norton.

Wittgenstein L. (1953). *Philosophical investigations*. Oxford: Blackwell.

Wittgenstein, L. (1965). *The blue and brown books*. New York: Harper Torchbooks.

Wittgenstein, L. (1980). *Culture and value*. Oxford: Blackwell.

Footnotes

[1] For purposes of this discussion, emotion and affect are not distinguished, nor is reference made to debates on the differences between them.

[2] Among the few exceptions are: on the Vygotsky side, Gonzalez Rey (1999, 2007), Smagorinsky (2011, 2012), and recent discussions of the Russian word "perezhi'vaniye," as a unity of personality and environment that are primarily taking place among a group of scholars on the Mind, Culture and Activity/xmca listserve (http://lchc.ucsd.edu/MCA/Mail/index.html); on the clinical practitioner side, narrative therapist White in his later years (2006) and Seikkula (1993, 2003). In addition, the theoretical writings of Shotter (1989, 1993, 2003, 2006) and the faculty of the Massey University online Discursive Therapies course designed by Andy Lock (http://therapy.massey.ac.nz) address emotion.

[3] Decades earlier, Cole and Scribner made a similar point, noting that Vygotsky's socio-cultural approach "represents an attempt to extend to the domain of psychology Marx's thesis that man has no fixed human nature but continually makes himself and his consciousness through productive activity" (Cole & Scribner, 1974, p. 31). This was not the Vygotsky that came to be known in educational circles, however.

[4] In addition to Gergen's voluminous writings on social constructionism (most recent are (K. J. Gergen, 2009; M. M. Gergen & K.J. Gergen, 2012), Shotter has been a leading theoretical voice in exploring the relational basis of human subjectivity and the "otherness" in human relations in general and, more recently, in psychotherapy, bringing into his work Wittgenstein, Vygotsky, Voloshinov and Bakhtin (e.g., Shotter, 1989, 2000, 2006). Lock and Strong are also prolific writers in this regard. Notably, their *Social Constructionism: Sources and Stirrings in Theory and Practice* (2010) includes a full chapter on Vygotsky. McNamee and Gergen's 1992 collection of essays, *Therapy as*

Big Ideas and Revolutionary Activity

Social Construction introduced relational, meaning-making and non-objective counseling and therapy practices that have come to be known as collaborative (Anderson, 1997; Anderson & Gehart, 2007), discursive (Pare & Larner, 2004; Strong & Lock, 2012; Strong & Pare, 2004), and narrative (McLeod, 1997; Monk, Winslade, Crocket, & Epston, 1997; Rosen & Kuehlwein, 1996; White, 2007; White & Epston, 1990).

5 In an essay historically situating certain of Vygotsky's ideas, Glick points out how English-language volumes of Vygotsky's work published at different times present a different Vygotsky, and a different zpd (Glick, 2004).

6 Wittgenstein is helpful in understanding the traps truth and cognition create in our language and thought. In his later works (1953, 1958), he exposed the "pathology" embedded in language and in accepted conceptions of language, thoughts and emotions. Some have described his work as therapeutic (Baker, 1992; van der Merwe and Voestermans, 1995), Newman and I among them.

We are all sick people, says Wittgenstein. No small part of what makes us sick is *how* we think (related in complicated ways to what we think and, even more fundamentally, to *that* we think or *whether* we think), especially how (that or whether) we think about thinking and other so-called mental processes and/or objects—something which we (the authors) think we (members of our culture) do much more than many of us like to think! It gets us into intellectual-emotional muddles, confusions, traps, narrow spaces; it torments and bewilders us; it gives us "mental cramps." We seek causes, correspondences, rules, parallels, generalities, theories, interpretations, explanations for our thoughts, words and verbal deeds (often, even when we are not trying to or trying not to). But what if, Wittgenstein asks, there are none? (Newman & Holzman, 2006/1996, p. 174).

This and subsequent quotations from social therapy clients are taken from an ongoing interview project.

Performing the World: The Emergence of Performance Activism

The Performance Turn in Social Change Activism

By Dan Friedman and Lois Holzman

Performing the World: The Performance Turn in Social Activism discusses the emergence of a new form of activism that is rooted in the human ability to perform. It introduces readers to the Performing the World (PTW) conference and the many political and social activists who have turned to the power of performance and its ability to engage and activate communities in the revolutionary practice of creating (and performing) new political, social and personal possibilities. The first PTW conference took place in 2001, and in the ensuing decades PTW has emerged as an international self-organizing community in which performance activists and scholars from around the world share the ways play and performance are being practiced to transform their communities. PTW focuses on topics such as the role of performance in youth development, the nature of social transformation and how we might achieve it, and co-creating ongoing dialogue between disciplines such as psychology, healthcare, education, community and youth development, and theatre and performance studies.

The performance turn is widely acknowledged. The premise that all (or much) of human practices are performed, that humans, through performance, function as the active social constructors of their world is not only embodied in the discipline of performance studies, but has become part of the dialogue in anthropology, linguistics, ethnography, folklore, psychology, sociology, and history. What is generally less recognized, both by scholars and by political activists themselves, is the performance turn in social activism.

The corruption and collapse of the Communist revolutions of the 20th century have called into question the value of ideology (in particular) and cognition and knowledge (in general) to provide a way out of the developmental dead ends—pervasive poverty, constant warfare and violence, the rapidly expanding gaps in wealth and opportunity—that appear to have trapped humanity. Acknowledging this, a growing number of political and social activists, community and youth organizers, progressive and critical educators and therapists, and others around the globe have been turning to performance as a way of engaging social problems, activating communities, and experimenting with new social and political possibilities. This shift looks different in different cultures and political environments. Whatever the differences, however, the

Big Ideas and Revolutionary Activity

performance shift is allowing social change activists in both modern and traditional cultures to organize not around a set of ideas, an ideology, but to create, through performance, something new with what exists. In our view, the performance turn has the potential to be socially and culturally transformative/revolutionary precisely because performance, consciously practiced in daily life, is, by its nature, a creative social activity that allows human beings to break out of old roles and old rules.

This chapter will focus on one manifestation of the performance turn, Performing the World (PTW), seven conferences that have taken place since 2001. PTW has served as a cross-disciplinary gathering of performance practitioners and scholars from every continent, many of them grassroots community organizers. It not only provides the opportunity for participants to learn from and inspire each other, but also to create informal international networks and collaborations. PTW has brought together a wide range of individuals, organizations, approaches and experiences and thus can provide a useful introduction to and overview of the performance phenomenon emerging around the world. Further, the unique origins of PTW in a radically humanistic, socio-cultural, therapeutic approach to human development and community organizing have given a particular shape to its contribution to the spread of performance activism.

In unpacking the origins and development of PTW and in analyzing the larger performance turn in social activism, the authors draw upon their insider position. Both are leaders of the performance community that initiated and organizes PTW and both have been engaged in performance activism for three decades. Holzman, a developmental psychologist, along with the late Fred Newman, is the founder and remains the key organizer of PTW. Friedman is the artistic director of the Castillo Theatre in New York City, and as such he has interfaced extensively with the theatre world relative to performance activism and scholarship.

Performance activism has a number of distinct, albeit related, origins. Theatre is one vital source—both political and educational theatre. Another source is the performance turn in psychology and the social sciences, part of the larger embrace of performance associated with some versions of postmodernism. A third is to be found in the grassroots community and political organizing led by Fred Newman and his colleagues in New York City beginning in the early 1970s.

Political and Experimental Theatre

We begin with political theatre, a term that itself has a myriad of meanings and reference points. Most relevant in regard to the emergence of performance activism, is political theatre as a mass amateur activity which emerged in the years immediately following World War I and the Russian Revolution in both Germany and the Soviet Union with the support and encouragement of the communist movement. Agit-prop troupes (short for agitation and propaganda) were made up of mostly urban workers who created and rehearsed short plays after work. The agit-prop plays were mobile, used few props or costume pieces, and consisted primarily of choral recitation, choreographed mass movement and stock, cartoon-like characters. They were performed primarily at political rallies, union and community meetings and on the streets. They flourished first in Germany and the Soviet Union and eventually in many other countries through the mid-1930s.

While they didn't survive the repression of the Nazis or Stalin's shifting cultural policy, the significance of the agit-prop movement in regard to this discussion is that it established that performance and theatre were creative activities that ordinary people could actively participate in. One didn't need intensive, specialized training to act or to create original theatre that embodied the lives, concerns and politics of its creators.

The political and cultural upheavals of the 1960s saw the re-emergence of amateur political theatre, this time created primarily by college students, again, primarily using public spaces—streets, student unions, and at rallies. One variant of sixties political theatre that pointed most clearly in the direction of what we are here calling performance activism was "guerrilla theatre," which consisted of staged conversations or actions done in public spaces in which the audience was unaware that it was watching or involved in a performance (for example, holding a loud performed conversation about the Vietnam War on a crowded subway car). Guerrilla Theatre purposely blurred the line between daily life and theatre/performance. The legacy of guerrilla theatre can be seen most clearly in groups like the Guerrilla Girls, Improv Everywhere and the Yes Men, as well as in the phenomena of flash mobs.

Two developments in the professional avant-garde of the late sixties also contributed to the loosening of the ties that had bound performance for so long to the institutional confines of the theatre.

One was environmental theatre, pioneered by Richard Schechner's Performance Group (1967-80). Environmental theatre is theatre that works to eliminate the distinction between the audience's and the actors' space. The performance takes place in, around, and among the audience in a shared space. Environmental theatre has had an ongoing impact on the aesthetics of mainstream theatre, most obviously in the hundreds of "site specific" theatre projects that take place every year in North America and Europe. The significance of this experimentation, which was influenced by Schechner's study of performance in tribal and traditional societies, is the expansion of the performance space beyond the stage. Schechner, not surprisingly, went on to help found performance studies.

Another development in the experimental theater of the sixties that helped to lay the groundwork for the performance turn in activism is what might be called the ritualization of theatre. Of course, all theatre, including the most "realist" is, on many levels, ritual. What we're referring to here are the efforts by the Living Theatre and others to transform the dynamic of the theatre from one in which actors perform a story to a passive audience, into one in which actors and audience both take part

Big Ideas and Revolutionary Activity

(mostly in prescribed ways) in a performed ritual. The performers thus function more as shamans than actors. The challenge here being that shamanism depends on a shared belief structure by all involved, not usually the case in the temporary community that comes into being for a night's performance in contemporary modern society. These experiments in ritualizing theatre can be traced back theoretically to the writing of Antonin Artaud and experientially to the mass demonstrations of the sixties. These demonstrations, mass performances enacted in streets, engendered a spirit of community among like-minded people through the ritualized performance of chanting, singing, and confronting police authority. Relative to the development of performance activism, these experiments helped to make clear (as agit-prop did a generation earlier) the possibility of performance by non-actors and to tie this conviction to a progressive politic.

Beyond these experiments in the theatre of the sixties, something must be said here about the pervasive and continuing impact of the sixties counter culture, which was profoundly performatory. Young people grew their hair and beards, put flowers in their hair and chose their costumes carefully, usually as a response to the conformism of middle class life. Many even changed their names. People were working to re-create/re-perform themselves and through this daily performance create new possibilities for themselves and the world. Indeed, we would argue that the overall politic of the counter culture was premised on the assumption that creating more growthful and cooperative performances—be that by living in communes or having non-monogamous, non-possessive sexual relationships—would impact on the larger society by example. However naïve that assumption, the lasting impact of trying to change the world by performing differently in daily life was not lost on those who would go on to create the performance activism of the Performing the World community.

Educational Theatre

In addition to political and experimental theatre, a second theatrical stream flowing into the emerging river of performance activism has been educational theatre. Like political theatre, educational theatre has many manifestations and meanings. Broadly speaking, it has come to refer to both the use of theatre as an educational tool in schools and the use of theatre to educate an audience outside the frame of formal educational institutions. In this latter sense educational theatre has given birth to Theatre for Development, a term used primarily in Africa and Asia, to describe explicitly didactic theatre produced to educate communities on subjects ranging from birth control and HIV/AIDS to agricultural techniques to gender violence, etc. Often this theatre work is funded by European based NGOs or religious organizations that see theatre as a tool in the arsenal of helping the poor country to "develop," hence the label.

Closely related to (and often overlapping with) educational theatre is "theatre for social change," a label more often used in the wealthy countries, particularly the United States, for theatre functioning at the grassroots level, often outside of formal theater buildings, with the goal of fostering social change. In some ways it is the contemporary manifestation of the agit-prop and street theatre traditions of the 20th century, although it is usually created by trained theatre artists who bring plays and/or the theatre making process into communities from the outside.

The most influential current within this stream is Theatre of the Oppressed in all its multiplying variations. Much has been written about Theatre of the Oppressed in this volume and elsewhere, and so we will be brief. In our view, Boal's most radical contribution relative to performance activism is the designation of audience members as "spec-actors," who are encouraged to intervene in the performance. While the Theatre of the Oppressed does not go as far as bringing performance off the stage into daily life, it does encourage the non-actor to take the stage. According to the Theatre of the Oppressed International Organization there are Theatre of the Oppressed groups active in 61 countries.

Another current in the mix of contemporary theatre for social change is Playback Theatre, founded in 1975 by Jonathan Fox and Jo Salas. Playback groups are now active in 50 countries. Playback uses improvisation to bring people's lived experiences directly onto the stage. Typically, it involves the actors asking audience members to share stories from their lives, sometimes related to trauma, which the actors then "playback," turning the stories into scenes on the spot. The improvised performances most often then lead to further discussion between the actors and the audience.

In recent years these various tendencies within educational theatre and theatre for social change—Theatre for Development, Theatre of the Oppressed, Playback Theatre and many other variants—have, for the most part, embraced a common identity as "Applied Theatre." The label refers to the common approach of *applying* theatre as a tool to teach, engage communities, spark conversations, etc. about social, political, educational and cultural issues. Many practitioners who identity with this label, and for whom applied theatre and theatre activism are synonymous, have made PTW their home over the past decade.

Performative Psychology

Another source of performance activism is the coming together of on-the-ground community organizing for progressive social change with the emergence of a performance turn within psychology and the other social sciences.

Among academics and practitioners critical of the social-scientific mainstream (on ethical, political and/or scientific grounds) who make a shift from a natural science based and individualistic approach to understanding human life to a more cultural and relational approach, some have come to understand human life as primarily performatory or performative. While these terms have different origins, senses and reference in different disciplines, today both terms broadly connote that people are performers and the world a series of "stages" upon which we create the millions of scripted and improvised scenes of our lives. Contrary to mainstream psychology's

Big Ideas and Revolutionary Activity

premise that the essential feature of human beings is our cognitive ability (often accompanied by a subordination of our affective ability), performative psychology puts performance "center stage." To performative theorists, researchers and practitioners, people's ability to perform—to pretend, to play, to improvise, to be who we are and "other" than who we are—is simultaneously cognitive and emotive. It is seen as an essential human characteristic, essential to our emotional-social-cultural-intellectual lives—but dramatically overlooked by mainstream psychology.

This shift has breathed new life into qualitative research within the social sciences, spawning the methodology known as "performative social science" or "performative inquiry." The methodology takes two directions: 1) a newly evolving method of inquiry/research (i.e., performative ways of doing social science) and 2) an alternative understanding and practice of relating to human beings (i.e., a practical-critical methodology based in the human capacity to perform).

Performance as a Method of Inquiry: Performing Social Science

The activity of developing alternative modes of communicating psychological concepts, research and practices originated in the work of Ken and Mary Gergen and a few other qualitative researchers. Today, such innovators can be found in more than a dozen countries. Performative inquiry/performative social science involves breaking out of the typical stodgy academic performance of text, graphs, tables and Power Points. As defined by the Gergens, performative social science is "the deployment of different forms of artistic performance in the execution of a scientific project. Such forms may include art, theater, poetry, music, dance, photography, fiction writing, and multi-media applications. Performance-oriented research may be presented in textual form, but also before live audiences, or in various media forms (film, photographs, websites)."

Central to this endeavor is the need to develop awareness among social scientists that making statements about psychological acts doesn't represent reality but rather is an expressive act. This draws upon the philosopher John Searle's now classic work, *Speech Acts: An Essay in the Philosophy of Language*, in which he highlighted the performative nature of language, i.e., that utterances perform various social functions over and above conveying content.

Performance as a New Ontology: People Perform Their Lives

The other direction performative inquiry takes is relating to people as performers by studying the human activity of performing in its endless varieties and by creating opportunities for people to perform in new ways. For example, there are practitioners who, recognizing the emotional and social growth that occurs when people create together theatrically on stage, use theatrical performance techniques in non-theatrical settings to support the expression of people's creativity and sociality in all areas of their lives. Included here are various nontraditional therapies, including psychodrama, social constructionist, collaborative and narrative approaches. There are also educators who have made this performance turn, becoming attentive to creativity as *socially performed* and learning itself as a creative activity. Some relate explicitly to teaching and learning as improvisational and develop performatory practices of student-teacher engagement.

It is this direction of performative psychology that was taken by the community we the authors are part of. We became convinced that performing in new ways is key to ongoing human development, and that ongoing human development is a necessary bi-condition of global cultural and political transformation. Our unique brand of performance activism links performance inextricably to human and community growth and development. PTW was born as an organizing tactic of this community, and so we now offer a brief intellectual history of its activities.

This community of activists began by working in the poorest communities of New York City in the 1970s and has gone on to organize middle class and wealthy people to work with us to support poor people to develop and provide leadership to the process of positive social change, free of government, corporate or university dependence. This organizing has led to, among many other things, the development of outside of school youth programs, a theatre, a research and training center, social therapy practices, independent electoral campaigns and organizations on a national, and increasingly, international stage.

In the course of nearly four decades of this work, we have come to an understanding of performance as a transformative, developmental activity. We understand performance to be the universal human capacity to be both who we are and who we are not at the same time. It is this ability, we believe, that allows human beings to develop beyond instinctual and socially patterned behavior. This understanding of performance changes the very nature of social change activism.

In coming to this understanding/practice of performance, our organizing experience was enriched by both Newman's training in analytical philosophy, the philosophy of science and the foundations of mathematics under the mentorship of Donald Davidson at Stanford University, and Holzman's training in developmental psychology, psycholinguistics and cultural-historical activity theory (the latter as a post-doc researcher at Michael Cole's Laboratory of Comparative Human Cognition at Rockefeller University)—and by the embrace by Newman, Holzman, et al of the early methodological writings of Marx, the later writings of Austrian philosopher Ludwig Wittgenstein, and the work of Soviet psychologist Lev Vygotsky.

From Marx we took his dialectical methodology and insistence that human beings are not isolated individuals: "As society itself produces man as man, so it is produced by him. Activity and mind are social in their content as well as in their origin: they are social activity and social mind."

Second, we took from Marx that the transformation of the world and of ourselves as human beings is one and the same task: "The coincidence of the changing of

Big Ideas and Revolutionary Activity

circumstances and of human activity or self-changing can be conceived and rationally understood only as revolutionary practice." Revolutionary practice, we came to understand from Marx, is not so much the organizing toward a specific goal as it is a new conception of method, a conception of method that involves a unity of human beings and the world we've created/are re-creating.

From Wittgenstein, we came to an understanding of the limitations of language, and by extension, of ideology. Wittgenstein, in his later work, created a radically new method of doing philosophy, one without foundations, premises, generalizations or abstractions. His work exposed "the pathology" embedded in language and in accepted conceptions of language, thoughts and emotions. These linguistic/philosophical pathologies permeate everyday life and create intellectual-emotional muddles, as people look for: causes, correspondences, rules, parallels, generalities, theories, interpretations, explanations for our thoughts, words and verbal deeds—even when we are not trying to or trying not to! Getting out of these traps, we gradually concluded, required something other than language. It required performance.

Vygotsky brought Marx to bear on issues of human, particularly childhood, development and learning and formulated Marx's dialectical method in the following manner:

> The search for method becomes one of the most important problems of the entire enterprise of understanding the uniquely human forms of psychological activity. In this case, the method is simultaneously prerequisite and product, the tool and the result of the study.

Continuing to build on Marx's dialectical method, Newman and Holzman expanded Vygotsky's statement of method and posited that human beings not only make and use tools but we also make new kinds of tools—*tool-and-result tools*. In fact, people develop through tool-and-result method. Vygotsky showed how little children become speakers of a language by playing language games with us, and in their pretend play. In both activities the tool or process, and result or product, come into existence together.

Vygotsky said; "In play it is as though a child is a head taller than he is. Play is a leading factor in development." He is telling us that in play, we are who we are *and* who we are becoming *at the same time*. He noted that children learn by playing with the adults and older children around them, creating performances of learning. Newman and Holzman building on this and looking at the organizing work being done by hundreds of their colleagues—in therapeutics, youth organizing, theatre building, independent politics—came to realize that human development happens, not just with children, but with people of all ages, when we relate to them as "a head taller," that is, as who they are becoming. Just as a baby and mother perform conversation before the baby speaks correctly, school age children can perform reading or math or science before they know how, and adults can learn how to run their world by performing power.

The babbling baby, the actor on the stage, the student in a school play, the researcher singing her data, and all of us—are capable of creating new performances of ourselves continuously if we choose to. That's our understanding of how development happens—through the social-cultural activity of people together creating new possibilities and new options for how to be in, relate to, understand and change the world, which, of course, includes ourselves.

Relating to each other "a head taller" than ourselves is what the performance community that created PTW does with thousands of inner-city children and adolescents, with people in emotional distress, with adults who want to learn to be better parents—with each other, with everyone. We all have the capacity to play as children do, to do what we do not yet know how to do, to be who we are and other than who we are at the same time. This is performance. Performing is taking what exists and creating something new out of it. This is our performance activism.

Our Performance Activism on the Ground

The theoretical work outlined above has been done under the aegis of the East Side Institute for Group and Short Term Psychotherapy (founded by Holzman and Newman) (http://www.eastsideinstitute.org), which has functioned as the conduit/interface between the community organizing and the performance turn in psychology and other social sciences. A non-profit education, research and training center located in New York City, the Institute has introduced and organized thousands of educators, mental health and medical workers, scholars and community organizers across the globe to the performance turn in general and the performance approach outlined here, through online and NYC-based courses, study and training programs, international events and scholarly writings. It is through the Institute that PTW was launched.

One key Institute activity is the ongoing research and extension of social therapy, which Newman began practicing and developing in the late 1970s. As the *Encyclopedia of Critical Psychology* (in press) describes it, "Like other radical therapies of the time in the U.S. and Great Britain, social therapy engaged the authoritarianism, sexism, racism, classism and homophobia of traditional psychotherapy. However, from its beginning, social therapy also rejected the conceptions of explanation, interpretation, the notion of an inner self (that therapists and clients need to delve into) and other dualistic and otherwise problematic foundations of traditional psychology."

From the beginning, social therapy has been a group therapy, in which building the ensemble, as distinct from analyzing the individual, is considered the curative, development activity. While its language was not, in its early days, performatory, the building of the group was always approached as a creative activity. The social therapist's task is to lead the group in discovering/creating a method of relating to emotional talk relationally rather than individualistically. Conversation becomes a collective meaning-making activity rather than a representation of "reality" or an expression of inner feelings. In this process people come to appreciate what (and

Big Ideas and Revolutionary Activity

that) they can create, and simultaneously to realize the limitations of trying to learn and grow individually. The traditional therapeutic question, "How are you (each individual) feeling?" transforms to "How well is the group performing its activity?" The parallels to a director leading the devising of a play are clear, and as social therapy advanced, its understanding (and the language) of performance came to the fore.

Out of the experience of social therapy—embracing its group-building activity based on conversation and improvisation—emerged social therapeutics, a methodological approach to organizing for social change and development in which human beings are related to as creators of their culture and ensemble performers of their lives. Increasingly, over the last two decades, social therapeutics has understood the core of its method to be performance and its core activity as that of bringing performance and play into daily life. The social therapeutic approach to learning and development is being used in therapy offices, clinics, hospitals, classrooms, after-school programs, workplaces, and communities worldwide, and it has informed the organizations, projects and productions of our performance community.

The All Stars Project (ASP) (http://www.allstars.org) has greatly expanded the social therapeutic performance approach. Founded in 1980 by Newman and developmental psychologist and community and political activist Lenora Fulani, the ASP is a non-profit almost totally funded by individual contributions. Under the leadership of Gabrielle L. Kurlander, who has been its president and CEO since 1990, the ASP has expanded from a local New York City talent show raising money on the streets to one of the leading youth development efforts in the United States. She has built a fundraising operation, based on building strong relationships and the active participation of donors, that has raised some $50 million for its performance-based programs, and interfaced with educators and policy makers. Among its activities are three free after-school youth programs, a university-style free school of continuing development for people of all ages, and the Castillo Theatre, an experimental community-based political theatre.

The oldest and largest of the ASP projects is the All Stars Talent Show Network (ASTSN), which is active in New York City, Newark, New Jersey, Chicago, Illinois and the San Francisco Bay Area in California. Starting as a modest event in church basements in the South Bronx in the early 1980s, today the ASTSN involves approximately 10,000 young people aged 5 to 25 each year who produce and perform in talent shows in high school auditoriums. These shows often involve hundreds of performers in scores of acts and audiences of up to 1,500 people from their communities. Each show involves an organizing process of street outreach, auditions (everyone gets in), workshops during which the young people devise skits, or create collective poems, or write and perform letters to historic figures and, in the process, have their understanding of performance deepened—and the show itself. Those who are not interested in performing on stage have the opportunity to perform the roles of stagehand, usher, sound technician and producer.

The Development School for Youth is a year-long training and enrichment program functioning in four U.S. cities in partnership with corporate executives to provide "cosmopolitanizing" business and cultural experiences, leadership training and paid internships to young people ages 16 to 21. The program gives working class youth the experience of trying out the performance of the business world, in the process discovering that they *can* create new performances, all kinds of new performances.

Youth Onstage! is the ASP's performance school and youth theatre. It provides young people with some of the tools of the theatre—most importantly, we think, improvisation and ensemble building—to make use of in their daily lives.

The most recent organizational project of this community is UX, a free school for adults, where the most popular courses are Improv for Everyone, Acting for Everyone and Public Speaking. In its first two years, it has had nearly 2,000 students, 80% of them overwhelmingly Black and Latino. What all of these programs and activities have in common is encouraging participants to build social ensembles within which they can perform (as distinct from simply behave) in their daily lives.

The Castillo Theatre (http://www.castillo.org) was founded in 1983 as a theatre for the activist community being organized in New York. From the beginning it was an attempt to give poor and working people a way of creating performances that reflected their lives and perspectives. Under the leadership of Newman, who served as its artistic director and playwright in residence from 1989 to 2005, Castillo became, more explicitly, a means of liberating performance from the constraints of the institution of the theatre. Newman's experience at Castillo as an actor, director and playwright also had significant impact on his understanding of performance as a transformative activity.

A Brief History of Performing the World

This is the context in which the Performing the World organizing activity and its conferences emerged, initially as a coming together of the academic turn to performance in psychology and other social sciences, represented by the Gergens, and the on-the-ground work of helping people to create new performances off stage, represented by Newman and Holzman.

Their first collaboration was the 1997 conference titled "Unscientific Psychology: Conversations with Other Voices" that the Institute hosted, and which featured the Gergens as well as other postmodern and critical psychologists. The idea was to explore whether and how postscientific and postmodern psychology could impact on the social and political issues facing the world's people. About 150 practitioners, academics and community activists from 17 countries attended; most of them were drawn to the topic because they themselves were experimenting with non-traditional approaches or developing critical alternative theories. The format was designed to create new kinds of conversations, mixing the usual academic fare with experimental experiential/performatory activities. On Day One, there were eight formal presentations by the Gergens,

Big Ideas and Revolutionary Activity

Newman, Holzman and other leading postmodern and critical psychologists. Day Two consisted of two kinds of performance: participants broke into three groups to pursue further the topics from Day One and to create performances out of their discussions and display them on the stage; and Newman led a workshop in which participants created and performed an improvised play based on their lives.

At the same time, as part of their experimentation using performance to present postmodern ideas to audiences of psychologists, the Gergens included Newman and Holzman in their Performative Psychology symposia at American Psychological Association (APA) Conventions in the late 1990s. These symposia included plays, several by Newman, poetry, dance, comedy and other performance genre, all addressing topics relevant to psychologists. Newman continued to write plays for presentation at APA conventions over the next few years.

The success of these ventures, coupled with the desire to bring performance activists together with performance scholars, led to the first PTW in 2001, co-sponsored by Newman's and Holzman's East Side Institute and the Gergens' Taos Institute. "Performing the World: Communication, Improvisation and Societal Practice" was held in the seaside village of Montauk, New York. It included theatre artists, dancers, performance studies academics and young people from the All Stars youth programs. Most of the 250 participants came from the US, with about two dozen from other countries. Since then, the Institute has continued organizing an international performance community of activists and scholars, and hosting PTW conferences— joining forces with the All Stars Project in 2008. Since that time, All Stars President Kurlander has served as PTW's co-executive producer with Holzman.

There has been both continuity and transformation over the seven PTW gatherings that have taken place between 2001 and 2012. The number of participants has doubled, and international presence has increased to more than 50%, with 35-40 countries now represented. The "performance politic" of the activists who launched PTW was there from the beginning, but it was more difficult to showcase when PTW was organized as a retreat in resort areas outside of New York City (in 2001, 2003, 2005, 2007). For one thing, the price of the conference, food and accommodations limited attendance to those who could afford it or had institutional funding, leaving out many activists and scholars from poorer countries, non-affiliated activists and ordinary New Yorkers. For another, the idyllic surroundings had their appeal but, at the same time, were, for the most part inaccessible to many activists and non-academics. In response to these limitations, in 2008 the Institute joined forces with the All Stars Project and moved the international gathering to the All Stars' headquarters in New York's theatre district.

In an announcement of the co-sponsorship, the Institute and the All Stars wrote:
> PTW '08 is bringing the international performance movement to the streets of New York—and introducing the performance movement to the communities of New York City. For the first time, the All Stars Project, an organization recognized for its highly successful performance-based outside-of-school developmental programs for young people and its Castillo Theatre, joins the East Side Institute as a co-sponsor of the conference. PTW '08 will be based out of the All Stars' performance and development center on 42nd Street near Times Square, and will be hosted by young people from around the city. Workshops and performances will take place there and at theatres, schools and other venues throughout Manhattan and other boroughs. New Yorkers from virtually every neighborhood will open up their homes to out-of-towners, not only to save on hotel costs, but also to incorporate the diversity of family and neighborhood into the experience of the weekend and to build person-to-person ties between ordinary New Yorkers and performance activists and scholars from around the world.

By this time, the international community of activist performers had grown substantially. Thousands were working in their communities with creative, performatory and dramaturgical approaches to social change, community empowerment, education, psychology, health and mental health, children's rights, trauma and violence, and more. The international performance movement that we had worked to nurture and shape since 2001 was poised to enter a much larger arena of international conversation on issues of citizenry, globalization, international poverty, humanitarianism, peace, sustainability, participation, collaboration, social entrepreneurship and cultural creativity. The Institute, All Stars and their broader performance activist community had something important to bring to these dialogues—perspectives and practices created outside of academia yet relevant to and recognized by the most progressive and nontraditional social science scholars, and hands-on experiences in "performing the world" as a necessary part of "transforming the world."

What made such engagement possible was the overall environment in which these gatherings of 400-500 people from dozens of countries took place. The diverse development community created by the All Stars and the Institute was the real host: nearly 200 volunteers—poor, working class and middle class young people and adults—staffed PTW; another 100+ across the five boroughs of New York City were housing hosts, providing attendees with a place to sleep (often a living room couch) and come home to each night. These experiences—for South African theatre professors, Brazilian teachers, youth workers from Peru, Park Avenue businessmen, unemployed mothers in Bed-Stuy, Brooklyn, non-profit managers in Manhattan's East Village, and high school students in Harlem—were not only once in a lifetime developmental moments for individuals, but were recognized as embodying the

Big Ideas and Revolutionary Activity

methodology of the community. As one participant wrote post PTW 2012: "The village of volunteers that you have is the best credit to the work and the philosophy of the organization that you represent."

In this environment, new kinds of conversations between and among diverse voices could be created, conversations that have continued and developed over the subsequent conferences. One example is a 2006 plenary session, "Ways of Performing Community," a conversation between grassroots builders and scholars from Brazil, India, South Africa and the U.S. The dialogue between the academy and grassroots activists, as well as between diverse cultures, remains an ongoing and deepening current within PTW.

Another current was first expressed in a public conversation between postmodern Marxist Newman and modernist Marxist Ian Parker, from Manchester Metropolitan University in the U.K., at which they explored their very different views on "What is Revolution?" This question, which touches on the nature of social transformation and the means of achieving it, also continues as a significant thread in the PTW tapestry.

The two major activities from which PTW participants have been drawn over the years—psychology and theatre—have been in dialogue throughout PTW's history. The plenary, "Theory/Practice: Culture and Psychology, Therapy and Theatre," in 2010 featured—among others—Woodie King, Jr., founding producing director of the New Federal Theatre, Judith Malina, founder and artistic director of the Living Theatre and Patch Adams, a medical doctor and pioneer of performance as therapeutic for the sick. The 2012 plenary, "The Therapeutic Power of Performance," featured seven leading play and performance activists and psychologists from Taiwan, France, Colombia and the US who explored with each other and the audience the developmental potential of the therapeutic turn in performance and the performance turn in therapy.

Another ongoing theme of PTWs has been the role of the performance approach to youth development, particularly poor youth and youth of color. PTW 2008 featured a plenary, "Performing Youth: A Conversation Across Borders," at which Lenora Fulani, a development psychologist and co-founder with Newman of the All Stars Project, led a public conversation with young people from New York, Johannesburg and Juarez. This was followed by an International Youth Talent Show, produced All Stars-style. PTW 2010 explored "The Performance of Blackness" through a mass theatrical performance, songs, raps and conversation involving scores of youth and adults organized and staged by Pam Lewis, the ASP's vice president of youth programs. In 2012, 78 PTW participants joined 200 hundred young people at their All Stars Talent Show Workshop in Harlem. In addition, youth organizers from nine countries participated in a pre-conference training in how to bring the All Stars Talent Show to their communities.

Perhaps most relevant to this volume has been the ongoing conversation between the academic discipline of Performance Studies and the social change methodology of performance activism. Although this conversation remains in its early stages (this chapter is, in fact, a part of that conversation), as early as 2008 Richard Schechner led a PTW session entitled, "The Performance of Studying Performance: Building Bridges Between the Academy and Performance Communities." In 2012, Schechner and one of us (Friedman) led a plenary on "What is Performance and How Do We Know It?" which was intended, "to challenge our Performance Studies scholars to study more actively and systematically the performance turn in social change organizing. ... and to challenge ... performance activists to actively invite that research and pursue what we can learn from it."

Many other conversations and variations of those touched on here take place at, around and between PTW conferences. Beyond the conferences themselves, they have generated exchanges, connections, and friendships among PTW participants and between housing hosts and participants. For example, as we were writing this, we received news that PTW participants from Johannesburg were planning to get together and talk. While PTW is a part of a much larger performance turn in social change activism, it has emerged as an important activity in helping that movement become aware of itself and is playing a leadership role in challenging the movement to embrace and deepen the transformational power of performance.

All of the PTWs have had titles. In 2010, we made its title the question that underlines performance activism—"Can Performance Change the World?" Two years later, with the world situation appearing even bleaker, we asked, "Can Performance ~~Change~~ Save the World?" Of course, these questions can't be answered in the abstract; in fact, they can't be answered at all. They can only be performed.

Endnotes

1 Carlson, Marvin, *Performance: A Critical Introduction*. New York: Taylor and Francis Group, 1996; Schechner, Richard, *Performance Studies: An Introduction*. London and New York: Routledge, 2002.

2 Newman, Fred, and Holzman, Lois, *The End of Knowing: A New Developmental Way of Learning*. London and New York: Routledge, 1997.

3 Friedman, Dan, 'Good-bye Ideology, Hello Performance,' *Topoi: An International Review of Philosophy*, Vol. 30, No. 2 (2011), pp. 125-35.

4 Bradshaw, Martha (ed.), Soviet Theater, 1917-1941. Ann Arbor: Edwards Bros., Inc., 1954; Carter, Huntly, *New Spirit in the Russian Theatre*, 1917-1928. New York: Brentano, 1929; Deak, Frantisek, 'Blue Blouse.' *The Drama Review*, Vol. 17, No. 9 (March 1973), pp.35-46; Houghton, Norris, *Moscow Rehearsals, An Account of Methods of Production in the Soviet Theatre*. London: Allen and Unwin, 1938; Hoffman, Ludwig and Hoffman-Ostwald, Daniel (eds). *Deutsches Arbeiter-theater, 1918-1933*, München: Rogner und Bernhard; Knellessen, Frederick Wolfgang,

Big Ideas and Revolutionary Activity

Agitation auf der Bühne: Das Politische Theater Der Weimarer Republik. Emsdetten: Verlag Lechte, 1970. Geddes, Virgil, *Left Turn for American Drama.* Brookfield, CT: Brookfield Players, 1934; Goldstein, Malcolm, *The Political Stage: American Drama and Theater of the Great Depression.* New York: Oxford University Press, 1974.

5 Guerrilla Girls, *Confessions of the Guerrilla Girls.* Perennial, 1995; Todd, Charlie, and Alex Scordelis, *Causing a Scene: Extraordinary Pranks in Ordinary Places with Improv for Everywhere.* New York: William Morrow, 2009; The Yes Men, *The Yes Men Fix the World*, DVD, 2009; Georgiana Gore, 'Flash Mob Dance and the Territorialisation of Urban Movement,' *Anthropological Notebooks*, Vol. 16, No.3, pp. 125-131, 2010.

6 Richard Schechner, *Essays on Performance Theory, 1970-1976.* New York: Drama Book Specialists, 1977.

7 Artaud, Antonin, translated by Mary Caroline Richards, *The Theatre and its Double.* New York: Grove Press, 1958.

8 www.theatreoftheoppressed.org/en/index.php?nodeID=2&category_id=17 (accessed 21 November 2012).

9 Dauber, Henrich, and Jonathan Fox (eds.), Gathering Voices: Essays on Playback Theatre, New Paltz, NY: Tusitala Publishers, 1999; Jo Salas, *Improvising Real Life: Personal Story in Playback Theatre.* New Paltz, NY: Tusitala, 1999.

10 Gergen, Kenneth J., and Mary M. Gergen, *Playing with Purpose: Adventures in Performative Social Science.* Walnut Creek, CA: Left Coast Press, 2012.

11 Holzman, Lois, *Performing Psychology: A Postmodern Culture of the Mind.* New York: Routledge, 1999; Newman, Fred, and Lois Holzman. The End of Knowing: *A New Developmental Way of Learning.* London; New York: Routledge, 1997.

12 Gergen, Kenneth J., *The Saturated Self: Dilemmas of Identity in Contemporary Life*, New York: Basic Books, 1991; Gergen, Mary M., *Feminist Reconstructions in Psychology, Narrative, Gender & Performance.* Thousand Oaks, CA: Sage, 2001.

13 Denzin, Norman K., 'The Reflexive Interview and a Performative Social Science,' *Qualitative Research*, 1, No. 1, (2001); Kip Jones, 'Connecting Research with Communities through Performative Social Science,' *The Qualitative Report*, Volume 17, Review/Essay 18, (2012) pp. 1-8, http://www.nova.edu/ssss/QR/QR17/jones.pdf (accessed 21 November 2012).

14 Gergen, Kenneth J., and Mary M. Gergen, 'Performative Social Science and Psychology,' FQS: *Forum: Qualitative Social Research* 12, No. 1 (2011), http://www.qualitative-research.net/index.php/fqs/article/view/1595 (accessed 21 November 2012).

15 Searle, John. *Speech Acts: An Essay in the Philosophy of Language.* Cambridge: Cambridge University Press, 1969.

16 McNamee, Sheila, and Kenneth J. Gergen, (eds.), Therapy as Social Construction. London: Sage, 1992; Moreno, J.L., and J. Fox, *The Essential Moreno: Writings in Psychodrama, Group Method, and Spontaneity.* New York: Springer Publishing

Selected Essays, Talks and Articles by Lois Holzman

Company, 1987; Neimeyer, R.A., and J.D. Raskin, 'Varieties of Constructivism in Psychotherapy' in *Handbook of Cognitive Behavioral Therapies (2nd Edition)*, edited by K. Dobson. pp.393-430. New York: Guilford, 2000; Newman, Fred, and Lois Holzman, "Beyond Narrative to Performed Conversation ('In the Beginning' Comes Much Later)," *Journal of Constructive Psychology* 12 (1999): pp. 23-40; Strong, Tom, and David Pare. *Furthering Talk: Advances in the Discursive Therapies*. New York: Kluwer Academic, 2004.

17 Lobman, Carrie, 'Improvising with(in) the System: Creating New Teacher Performances in Inner City Schools,' in Keith Sawyer (ed.), *The Teaching Paradox: Creativity in the Classroom*, Cambridge: Cambridge University Press, in press; Sawyer, Keith, *The Teaching Paradox: Creativity in the Classroom*. Cambridge: Cambridge University Press, in press.

18 Holzman, Lois, *Schools for Growth: Radical Alternatives to Current Educational Models*. Mahwah NJ: Lawrence Erlbaum Associates, 1997; Lobman, Carrie, and Barbara E O'Neill, (eds). Play and Performance, Vol. 11, Play & Culture Studies. New York: University Press of America, 2011; Martinez, Jaime E., *A Performatory Approach to Teaching, Learning and Technology*. Rotterdam, The Netherlands: Sense Publishers, 2011.

19 Newman, Fred, and Lois Holzman, *Unscientific Psychology: A Cultural-Performatory Approach to Understanding Human Life*. Lincoln, NE: iUniverse Inc. (originally published Westport, CT: Praeger), 2006/1996; Newman, Fred, and Lois Holzman, *The End of Knowing: A New Developmental Way of Learning*. London; New York: Routledge, 1997.

20 Friedman, Dan, 'Castillo: The Making of a Postmodern Political Theatre' in John W. Frick (ed.), *Theatre at the Margins: the Political, the Popular, the Personal, the Profane*. Tuscaloosa, AL: University of Alabama Press, 2000; Holzman, Lois, Vygotsky at Work and Play. New York: Routledge, 2009; Newman, Fred, Performance of a Lifetime; a Practical-Philosophical Guide to the Joyous Life. New York: Castillo International, 1996.

21 Marx, Karl, 'Economic and Philosophical Manuscripts' in E. Fromm (ed.), *Marx's Concept of Man*, New York: Frederick Ungar, 1967.

22 Marx, Karl, and F. Engels, 'Theses on Feuerbach' in *The German Ideology*. New York: International Publishers, 1974.

23 Newman, Fred and Lois Holzman, 'All Power to the Developing,' *Annual Review of Critical Psychology*, Vol. 3, (2003), pp. 8-23, http://www.discourseunit.com/annual-review/arcp-3-anti-capitalism/ (accessed 29 November 2012); Newman, Fred, and Lois Holzman, *Lev Vygotsky: Revolutionary Scientist*. London: Routledge, 1993.

24 Wittgenstein, Ludwig, *Philosophical Investigations*. Oxford: Blackwell, 1953; Wittgenstein, Ludwig, *The Blue and Brown Books*. New York: Harper Torchbooks, 1965.

[25] Newman, Fred, and Lois Holzman, *Unscientific Psychology: A Cultural-Performatory Approach to Understanding Human Life*. Lincoln, NE: iUniverse Inc. (originally published Westport, CT: Praeger), 2006/1996.

[26] Vygotsky, Lev S., Mind in Society. Cambridge MA: Harvard University Press, 1978; Vygotsky, Lev S., *The Collected Works of L.S. Vygotsky, Volumn 1, Problems of General Psychology*. New York: Plenum, 1987; Rieber, R.W., David Keith Robinson and Jerome S. Bruner (eds.), The Essential Vygotsky. New York: Kluwer Academic/Plenum Publishers, 2004.

[27] Vygotsky, Lev S., *Mind in Society*. Cambridge MA: Harvard University Press, 1978.

[28] Vygotsky, Lev S., *Mind in Society*. Cambridge MA: Harvard University Press, 1978.

[29] Newman, Fred, and Lois Holzman, *Lev Vygotsky: Revolutionary Scientist*. London: Routledge, 1993.

[30] Teo, Thomas (ed) *Encyclopedia of Critical Psychology*. SpringerReference.com, in press; Newman, Fred, 'A Therapeutic Deconstruction of the Illusion of Self' in Lois Holzman (ed.), *Performing Psychology: A Postmodern Culture of the Mind*, New York; Routledge, 1999, pp.111-32; Holzman, Lois, and Rafael Mendez, *Psychological Investigations: A Clinician's Guide to Social Therapy*. New York: Brunner-Routledge, 2003.

[31] Holzman, Lois, *Vygotsky at Work and Play*. New York: Routledge, 2009; Holzman, Lois, and Rafael Mendez. *Psychological Investigations: A Clinician's Guide to Social Therapy*. New York: Brunner-Routledge, 2003.

[32] Holzman, Lois, and John Morss (eds.), *Postmodern Psychologies, Societal Practice and Political Life*. New York: Routledge, 2000.

[33] Holzman, Lois, and John Morss (eds.), *Postmodern Psychologies, Societal Practice and Political Life*. New York: Routledge, 2000.

[34] Gergen, Kenneth J., and Mary M. Gergen, Playing with Purpose: *Adventures in Performative Social Science*. Walnut Creek, CA, Left Coast Press, 2012; Friedman, Dan (ed.), *Still on the Corner and Other Postmodern Political Plays by Fred Newman*, New York: Castillo Cultural Center, 1998.

[35] www.performingtheworld.org (accessed 21 November, 2012).

[36] See Performing the World website (www.performingtheworld.org) and the East Side Institute's Vimeo (http://vimeo.com/search?q=east+side+institute) channel for videos of some conference sessions.

[37] Friedman, Dan, 'Performance Studies/Performance Activism.' Paper presented at PTW 2012, October 4-7, 2012, New York City.

Without Creating ZPDs There is No Creativity

Without Creating ZPDs There Is No Creativity focuses on how groupings of people create environments in which qualitative transformation can take place. Offering her insights on several misconceptions present in more traditional applications of Lev Vygotsky's zones of proximal development (ZPDs), Lois asserts that in order for the ZPD to be an activity in which learning leads development, creativity, imitation, completion and play must be present. Creativity, understood as a social activity, is our ability to transform our determining environments, make new meanings and reshape our relationships to ourselves and to each other. Imitation, understood as a social activity, is our ability to imitate what is beyond ourselves by learning from those more experienced than we are, much like children do when playing house or doctor. Completion within the ZPD focuses on the dialectical movement of thought and speech in which speaking completes thinking. The social significance of completion is that in historical-sociocultural space, other people can complete for us, opening us up to possibilities we may not otherwise have entertained. Play is an activity where both old and new possibilities exist in the environment together, where we can "try on" new ways of thinking and doing, and this enables us to perform new versions of ourselves or as Vygotsky might say, be "a head taller" than we are.

When discussing the essential role of play in early child development, Vygotsky remarked, "In play a child always behaves beyond his average age, above his daily behavior; in play it is as though he were a head taller than himself" (1978, p. 102). In this chapter I will explore that marvelous metaphor "a head taller" in the context of investigating the mundane creativity that is and produces human development and learning. In other words, my focus here is on the *collective activity of creating*. I am interested in how social units create environments in which they qualitatively transform themselves and their environments. I propose an understanding of creativity as socially imitative and completive activity. I have come to this understanding from immersion in a quarter-century of intervention research that actualizes the "head taller" experience for people across the lifespan by allowing, inviting and guiding them to create zones of proximal development (ZPDs). This research, serving only as a backdrop for the present discussion, is discussed in other writings, the most recent being *Vygotsky at Work and Play* (Holzman, 2009).

A ZPD is a ZPD — or is it?

Even though Vygotsky's ZPD is essential to his understanding of *the relationship between development and learning and play*, it has become, in our time, more narrowly associated with learning and the school-like acquisition of knowledge and

Big Ideas and Revolutionary Activity

skills. Part of what I want to do in this discussion is restore the complexity, radicalness and practicality of Vygotsky's discovery of the ZPD.

The ZPD is important in Vygotsky's rejection of the popular belief that learning follows and is dependent upon development, and in his related criticism of traditional teaching: "Instruction would be completely unnecessary if it merely utilized what had already matured in the developmental process, if it were not itself a source of development" (Vygotsky, 1987, p. 212).[1] Rejecting the view that learning depends on and follows development, Vygotsky put forth a new relationship between these two activities: "The only instruction which is useful in childhood is that which moves ahead of development, that which leads it" (p. 211)... "pushing it further and eliciting new formations" (p. 198). In other words, for Vygotsky *learning leads development*. In previous works, I refer to this discovery as not merely a new relationship but as a new *kind* of relationship (at least for psychology)—the dialectical unity learning-leading-development. I do this to capture the way Vygotsky sees learning and development as a totality, and change as qualitative transformation of the whole (Holzman, 1997; Newman & Holzman, 1993).

The question of how learning leads development depends, at least in part, on how we understand what the ZPD is. As the most popularized concept stemming from Vygotsky's writings, the ZPD has been given multiple interpretations by educational researchers, psychologists and others. Different meanings can be traced, in part, to different translations of his writings (Glick, 2004) and from the numerous contexts in which Vygotsky wrote about the ZPD. In briefly reviewing some of these contexts, understandings and implications that follow from them, I will bring together Vygotsky's comments from diverse sources and provide the backdrop for the view I am putting forth.

Individual

A common understanding of the ZPD is that it is a characteristic or property of an individual child. This understanding stems from passages like the following:

> The psychologist must not limit his analysis to functions that have matured. He must consider those that are in the process of maturing. If he is to fully evaluate the state of the child's development, the psychologist must consider not only the actual level of development but *the zone of proximal development*. (Vygotsky, 1987, pp. 2018-209)

To some educational researchers this translates into the ZPD being—or producing—a measure of a child's potential, and they have devised alternative means of measuring and evaluating individual children (for example, Allal & Pelgrims, 2000; Lantolf, 2000; Lidz & Gindis, 2003; Newman, Griffin & Cole, 1989; Tharp & Gallimore, 1988).

Dyadic

In other passages, however, the ZPD plays a key role in Vygotsky's argument that learning and development are fundamentally social and form a unity. Joint activity and collaboration in children's daily life are also implicated, as in the following passage:

> What we call the Zone of Proximal Development ...is the distance between the actual developmental level as determined by independent problem solving, and the level of potential development as determined through problem solving under guidance or in collaboration with more capable peers. (Vygotsky, 1978, p. 86)

Perhaps it was the phrase "more capable" that led to the conceptualization of the ZPD as a form of aid—termed prosthesis by Shotter (1989) and Wertsch (1991) and scaffolding by Wood, Bruner and Ross (1976). [2] This conceptualization has become so popular that the typical college textbook equates the ZPD with scaffolding and (incorrectly) attributes both terms to Vygotsky (for example, Berk & Winsler, 1995; MacNaughton & Williams, 1998; Rodgers & Rodgers, 2004). Moreover, despite Vygotsky's mention of "peers" in the passage above, most empirical research with this perspective takes "the aid" to be a single, more capable individual, most often an adult (termed "expert" in contrast to the "novice" child).

In keeping with this dyadic interpretation of the ZPD, it is common for "social level" and "interpsychological" to be reduced to a two-person unit in the following oft-quoted passage:

> Every function in the child's cultural development appears twice: first on the social level and later, on the individual level; first *between* people *(interpsychological)*, and then *inside* the child *(intrapsychological)*. This applies equally to all voluntary attention, to logical memory, and to the formation of concepts. All the higher mental functions originate as actual relations between people. (Vygotsky, 1978, p. 57)

Collective

At other times Vygotsky emphasized more clearly that the socialness of learning-leading-development is collective, that the ZPD is not exclusively or even primarily a dyadic relationship, and that what is key to the ZPD is that people are doing something together. For example, "Learning awakens a variety of internal developmental processes that are able to operate only when the child is interacting with people in his environment and in cooperation with his peers" (Vygotsky, 1978, p. 90).

The necessity of collective activity that Vygotsky attributes to the learning-development relationship is at the forefront of his approach to special education. His writings on this subject (collected and published in English as *Fundamentals of Defectology*, 1997) argue that children with abnormalities such as retardation, blindness or deafness can indeed develop. They should not be written off or remediated, nor should these children be segregated and placed in schools with only children like themselves. Vygotsky made the point that qualitative transformation (as opposed to rote learning) is a collective accomplishment--a "collective form of 'working together'" he called it in an essay entitled, "The Collective as a Factor in the Development of the Abnormal Child" (Vygotsky, 2004, p. 202). In this same essay he characterized the social, or interpsychological, level of development (in the quote above, p. 4) as "a function of collective behavior, as a form of cooperation or cooperative activity" (p. 202).

I like that phrase, "a collective form of working together." It seems a good fit with my experience as researcher, teacher and trainer. I read Vygotsky here as saying that the *ZPD is actively and socially created*. This is beyond and perhaps other than the popular conception of the ZPD as an entity existing in psychological-cultural-social space and time. For me, the ZPD is more usefully understood as a process rather than as a spatio-temporal entity, and as an activity rather than a zone, space or distance. Furthermore, I offer the *ZPD activity* as the simultaneous creating of the zone (environment) and what is created (learning-leading-development).

Creativity

The concept of ZPD activity provides a new way to understand human development that puts creativity center stage. Not creativity as typically understood, however. For in both everyday and psychological discourse creativity is taken to be an attribute of individuals. Further, creative individuals are understood to produce special things — original, novel, unique, and perhaps extraordinary or extraordinarily significant — relative to others who are "not creative." The kind of creativity I am talking about in relation to ZPD activity is not an attribute of individuals but of social units (e.g., dyads, groups, collectives, and so on), and it is not special or extraordinary, but ordinary and everyday. (Yet, while mundane, it is also magical!)

How do social units create ZPDs? For one thing, we must be capable of doing what we do not know how to do, either individually or collectively. Human beings learn and develop without knowing how or that we know. In other words, *we become epistemologists without employing epistemology*. Vygotsky recognized this seeming paradox of human life, at least in its early childhood version. He understood that developmental activity does not require knowing how, as when he identified "the child's potential to move from what he is able to do to what he is not" (Vygotsky, 1987, p. 212) as the central characteristic and creative activity of learning leading development.

Further, he understood that for young children, knowing how to do a particular thing does not require knowing that they are doing this particular thing. As he put it,

"...before a child has acquired grammatical and written language, he knows how to do things but does not know that he knows.... In play a child spontaneously makes use of his ability to separate meaning from an object without knowing that he is doing it, just as he does not know he is speaking in prose but talks without paying attention to the words" (Vygotsky, 1978, p. 99). This thread of Vygotsky's thought has, to my way of thinking, been neglected, not only in the study of early childhood but also in its implications for understanding and fostering development throughout the lifespan If children do not need to know, why do the rest of us? (Holzman, 1997; Newman & Holzman, 1997). This question has been debated vigorously by postmodernists, of course, but very little by cultural historical activity theorists—a situation I have tried to remedy (see, for example, Holzman, 2006).

Inspired by Vygotsky's insights on how very young children and children with disabilities go beyond themselves qua selves and participate in ZPD activity (creating environments for learning-leading development and simultaneously learning-leading-development), my work has been to expand this creative methodology through collaboration with others in building "ZPD-creating-head taller"" therapeutic, educational and organizational practices and simultaneously studying the practices we have built. Development, from this perspective, is the practice of a *methodology of becoming* — in which people shape and reshape their relationships to themselves, each other and to the material and psychological tools and objects of their world.

Imitation

Thus far, I have suggested that from a developmental and educational perspective it is useful to understand ZPDs as actively created, that the creators are social units rather than individuals, and that the creative ZPD activity is a non-epistemological methodology of becoming. What is this methodology? In other words, what does being a head taller look like?

The answer requires taking a new look at imitation. Along with not knowing, imitation has been overlooked by socio-cultural researchers, in my opinion. And as with not knowing, I suggest that imitation is necessary for creativity in general and for creating ZPDs in particular. In relation to ZPDs, I take my cue from Vygotsky: "A full understanding of the concept of the zone of proximal development must result in a reevaluation of the role of imitation in learning" (1978, p. 87).

As part of his reevaluation, Vygotsky discounted an essentially mechanistic view of imitation that was "rooted in traditional psychology, as well as in everyday consciousness" (Vygotsky, 1987, p. 209). He was also wary of the individualistically biased inferences drawn from such a view, as for example, that "the child can imitate anything" and that "what I can do by imitating says nothing about my own mind" (1987, p. 209). In its stead, Vygotsky posited that imitation is a social-relational activity essential to development: "Development based on collaboration and imitation is the source of all specifically human characteristics of consciousness that develop in a child" (Vygotsky, 1987, p. 210).

Children do not imitate anything and everything as a parrot does, but rather what is "beyond them" developmentally speaking and yet present in their environment and relationships. In other words, imitation is fundamentally creative, by which I mean that it helps to create the ZPD. The kind of language play that typifies conversations

Big Ideas and Revolutionary Activity

between very young children and their caregivers can perhaps provide clarity on this point. Here is one of Vygotsky's many descriptions of early childhood language development. It is a difficult passage, one that I have to re-discover the meaning of each time I read it.

> We have a child who has only just begun to speak and he pronounces single words… But is fully developed speech, which the child is only able to master at the end of this period of development, already present in the child's environment? It is, indeed. The child speaks in one-word phrases, but his mother talks to him in language which is already grammatically and syntactically formed and which has a large vocabulary… Let us agree to call this developed form, which is supposed to make its appearance at the end of the child's development, the final or ideal form. And let us call the child's form of speech the primary or rudimentary form. The greatest characteristic feature of child development is that this development is achieved under particular conditions of interaction with the environment, where this …form which is going to appear only at the end of the process of development is not only already there in the environment … but actually interacts and exerts a real influence on the primary form, on the first steps of the child's development. *Something which is only supposed to take shape at the very end of development, somehow influences the very first steps in this development.* (Vygotsky, 1994, p. 348)

Both developed and rudimentary language are present in the environment, Vygotsky tells us. In that case, what is environment? If both forms of language are present, then environment cannot be something fixed in space and time, nor separate from child and mother. Rather, it seems that environment must be both what is—the specific socio-cultural-historical conditions in which child and mother are located—and what is coming into existence—the changed environment being created by their language activity. In other words, this environment is as much activity as it is context. In their speaking together, very young children and their caregivers are continuously reshaping the "rudimentary" and "developed" forms of language. It is this activity, I suggest, that is and creates the ZPD—and through which the child develops as a speaker, meaning maker and language user.

Completion

Along with imitation there is another activity taking place in the creating of the language-learning ZPD—completion. This idea is based in Vygotsky's understanding of the relationship between thinking and speaking, in which he challenged the expressionist view of language (that our language expresses our thoughts and feelings). Speaking, he said, is not the outward expression of thinking, but part of a unified, transformative process. Two passages from *Thinking and Speech* are especially clear in characterizing his alternative understanding:

> The relationship of thought to word is not a thing but a process, a movement from thought to word and from word to thought ... Thought is not expressed but completed in the word. We can, therefore, speak of the establishment (i.e., the unity of being and nonbeing) of thought in the word. Any thought strives to unify, to establish a relationship between one thing and another. Any thought has movement. It unfolds. (Vygotsky, 1987, p. 250)

> The structure of speech is not simply the mirror image of the structure of thought. It cannot, therefore, be placed on thought like clothes off a rack. Speech does not merely serve as the expression of developed thought. Thought is restructured as it is transformed into speech. It is not expressed but completed in the word. (Vygotsky, 1987, p. 251)

Instead of positing a separation into two realms—the private one of thinking and the social one of speaking—there is just one: speaking/thinking, a dialectical unity in which speaking *completes* thinking. Vygotsky was delineating the thinking-speaking process for individuals, but his conceptualization can be expanded in the following way. If speaking is the completing of thinking, if the process is continuously creative in socio-cultural space, then the "completer" does not have to be the one who is doing the thinking. Others can complete for us (Holzman, 2009; Newman & Holzman, 1993). Think about it. Would children be able to engage in language play/conversation before they knew language if thinking/speaking were not a continuously socially completive activity in which others were completing for them?

The ongoing activity of completion can be seen in the conversations that very young children and their speaking caregivers create, as in caregivers' typical responses to the single words and phrases of toddlers (e.g., Child: "Cookie!" Adult: "Want a cookie?" [getting cookie and giving it to child] Child: "Mama cookie." Adult: "Yes, Mommy's giving you a cookie."). Like the child's imitations, completion is also a dominant activity of creating the language-learning ZPD.[3] Together, imitation and completion comprise much of the language play that transforms the total environment, a process out of which a new speaker emerges.

The current culture too often loses sight of what I have presented—not its detail but its general common sense notions. Children do not learn language, nor are they taught language in the structured, systematic, cognitive, acquisitional and transmittal sense typical of later institutionalized learning and teaching. They develop as speakers, language makers and language users as an inseparable part of joining and transforming the social life of their family, community and culture. When babies begin to babble they are speaking before they know how to speak or that they speak, by virtue of the speakers around them accepting them into the community of speakers and creating conversation with them. Mothers, fathers, grandparents, siblings and others do not have a curriculum, give them a grammar book and dictionary to study,

Big Ideas and Revolutionary Activity

nor remain silent around them. Rather, they relate to infants and babies as capable of doing things that are beyond them. They relate to them as fellow speakers, feelers, thinkers and makers of meaning—in other words, as fellow creators. This is what makes it possible for very young children to be as though a head taller.

Play

It is time to return to play, the activity to which Vygotsky attributed the "head taller" experience. His writing on play concerned young children's free play of fantasy and pretense, and the more structured and rule-governed playing of games that becomes frequent in later childhood.

All play, Vygotsky believed, creates an imaginary situation and all imaginary situations contain rules. It is the relationship between the two that changes with different kinds of play. In the game play of later childhood, rules are overt, often formulated in advance, and dominate over the imaginary situation. The elements of pretend are very much in the background and rules are instrumentally necessary to the playing (Vygotsky, 1978). Think of basketball, video games and board games.

In the earlier play of very young children—the rich meaning-making environment of free and pretend play—the imaginary situation dominates over rules. The rules don't even exist until the playing begins, because they come into existence at the same time and through the creation of the imaginary situation. In Vygotsky's words, they are "not rules that are formulated in advance and that change during the course of the game but ones that stem from an imaginary situation" (1978, p. 95). That is, they are rules created *in the activity of playing*.

When a young child takes a pencil and makes horse-like movements with it, in creating this imaginary situation s/he is simultaneously creating the "rules" (keep jumping, make whinnying sounds, don't write on the paper) of the play. When children are playing Mommy and baby, the new meaning that the imaginary situation creates also creates the "rules" of the play (for example, how Mommy and baby relate to each other "in character"). In these examples, at the same time as new meaning is being created with pencil, self and peer, the "old" meanings of horse, pencil, Mommy and baby are suspended from these objects and people. Both the old and the new meanings are present in the environment. This is analogous to creating language-learning ZPDs just discussed, in which environment is both the specific socio-cultural-historical conditions under which children play, and the changed environment being created by their play activity. Here, as in that case, environment is as much activity as it is context.

It is these elements of free or pretend play that, for Vygotsky, distinguish the play ZPD from that of learning-instruction ZPD:

> Though the play-development relationship can be compared to the instruction-development relationship, play provides a much wider background for changes in needs and consciousness. Action in the imagina-

tive sphere, in an imaginary situation, the creation of voluntary intentions, and the formation of real-life plans and volitional motives—all appear in play and make it the highest level of preschool development. (Vygotsky, 1978, pp. 102-103)

In making this distinction, to my way of thinking Vygotsky makes too sharp a break between playing and learning-instruction. Can't play be the highest level of preschool development and still be developmentally important across the life span? I think so. I think that Vygotsky overlooked some continuity between the two ZPDs, in part because he was so concerned with learning in formalized school contexts. This continuity, which I have come to believe have significance for later childhood and beyond, relates to the characteristics of creativity in ZPD activity that I have been discussing.

Learning Playfully Outside of School

It is a feature of our western culture (and most other cultures) that we relate to very young children as creative. I mean that both in the sense of creativity I have introduced here —their participation in creating ZPDs—and in the more conventional sense of appreciating their individual products (scribbles, phrases, songs, dances, and so on). And we gradually stop doing so as they get older. We bifurcate learning and playing, trivializing play in the process, and have created institutionalized structures to maintain that bifurcation and trivialization. We introduce the concept of work. In nearly all schools the elements of ZPD-creating—freedom from knowing, creative imitation, and completion— are absent.

We also relate to the imitative activity of very young children as creative in both the mundane and the appreciative senses. And we gradually stop doing that as they get older. Imitating becomes copying. What once gave delight is to be avoided. A child of three or four years is likely to be told she is clever or smart (or at least cute) for creatively imitating. In nearly all schools, a child of seven or eight is likely to be told she is cheating and shouldn't copy.

In the extreme, schooling transforms not knowing into a deficit; creative imitation into individualized accomplishments; rote learning and testing; and completion into correction and competition.

This is the current situation. This is what schools do and don't do. I am as concerned as the next person about it, but I am equally concerned with bringing outside-of-school learning to the forefront of dialogue and debate among educators, researchers, policy makers and the public. This is because that is where creativity still lives. Putting on a play or concert and playing basketball as a team require the members to create a collective form of working together. Unfortunately, doing well in school does not. My reading of the literature on outside-of-school programs, along with my own intervention research, shows that outside-of-school programs (in particular, those involving

Big Ideas and Revolutionary Activity

the arts or sports) are more often than not learning-leading-development environments, methodologically analogous to early childhood ZPDs in a manner appropriate to school-aged children and adolescents.[4] Whether deliberately or not, they continue to relate to young people as creative, in both mundane and appreciative senses.

These kinds of cultural outside-of-school programs share important features, most notably, those that foster activities that create ZPDs: freedom from knowing and socially imitative and completive activity. First, kids come to them to learn how to do something they do not know how to do. Maybe they want to perform in a play, make music videos, play the flute, dance, or play basketball. They bring with them some expectation that they *will* learn. They are related to by skilled outside-of-school instructors, often practitioners themselves, as capable of learning, regardless of how much they know coming into the program. Thus, while there are of course differences in skills and experience that young people bring to outside-of-school programs, the playing field is more level than in school. Really good programs, in fact, use such heterogeneity for everyone's advantage (Gordon, Bowman, & Mejia, 2003; Holzman, 2006, 2009).

Second, in these programs it's OK to imitate and complete. In fact, it's essential. The presumption is that how one becomes an actor, music producer, musician, dancer and athlete is by doing what others do and building on it. From the fundamentals through advanced techniques and forms, creatively imitating instructors and peers — and being completed by them— is what is expected and reinforced.

I have come to view outside-of-school programs that have these features as learning environments created by, and allowing for, *learning playfully*. They are, in this sense, a synthesis of Vygotsky's ZPDs of learning-instruction and of play, not as spatio-temporal zones but as mundane creative activity. For, as in the free or pretend play of early childhood, the players (both students and instructors) are more directly the producers of their environment-activity, in charge of generating and coordinating the perceptual, cognitive and emotional elements of their learning and playing. Most psychologists and educators value play for how it facilitates the learning of social roles, with socio-cultural researchers taking play to be an instrumental tool that mediates between the individual and the culture and, thereby, a particular culture is appropriated (as in the work of Nicolopoulou & Cole, 1993; Rogoff, 1990; Rogoff & Lave, 1984; Wertsch, 1985). Through acting out roles (play-acting), children try out the roles they will soon take on in "real life." I am sympathetic to this understanding and yet I think there is more that play contributes to development than this. Being a head taller is an ensemble performance, not "an act." After all, we don't say the babbling baby is acting out a role.

I see play as both appropriating culture and creating culture, a performing of who we are becoming (Holzman, 1997, 2009; Newman & Holzman, 1993). I see creative imitation as a type of performance. When they are playing with language very young children are simultaneously performing—*becoming*—themselves. In the theatrical sense of the word, performing is a way of taking "who we are" and creating something new—in this case a newly emerging speaker, on the stage a newly emerging character, in an outside of school program a skilled dancer or athlete—through incorporating "the other."

In his essay on the development of personality and world view in children, Vygotsky wrote that the preschool child "can be somebody else just as easily as he can be himself" (Vygotsky, 1997, p. 249). Vygotsky attributed this to the child's lack of recognition that s/he is an "I" and went on to discuss how personality and play transform through later childhood. I take Vygotsky to be saying that performing as someone else is an essential source of development, at the time of life before "I." Early childhood is the time before "I" and the time before "I know." We can never completely replicate the type of lived activity out of which learning-leading-development occurs and "I" and "I know" are created. Nor should we want to. But outside of school programs, to the extent that they are spaces and stages for creativity (mundane and otherwise), appear to support young people's learning-leading-development through revitalizing play and performance. Such programs are precisely the kind of support schools need, for as long as schools continue to discourage creativity.

References

Allal, L. & Pelgrims, A. (2000). Assessment of or in the zone of proximal development. *Learning and Instruction*, 10(2), 137-152.

Arts Education Partnership (1999). *Champions of change: The impact of the arts on learning*. Washington, DC: Arts Education Partnership.

Berk, L. E. & Winsler, A. (1995). *Scaffolding children's learning: Vygotsky and early childhood education*. Washington, DC: National Association for the Education of Young Children.

Carnegie Council on Adolescent Development (1992). *A matter of time: Risk and opportunity in the nonschool hours*. Carnegie Council Monograph. Retrieved from http://www.carnegie.org/ccadpubs.htm.

Childress, H. (1998). Seventeen reasons why football is better than high school. Phi Delta Kappan. 79(8), 616-620.

Glick J. (2004). The history of the development of higher mental function. In R.W. Rieber & D. K. Robinson (Eds.), *The essential Vygotsky*. NY: Kluwer Academic/Plenum Publishers.

Gordon, E. W., Bowman, C.B. & Mejia, B. X. (2003). *Changing the script for youth development: An evaluation of the All Stars Talent Show Network and the Joseph A. Forgione Development School for Youth*. Institute for Urban and Minority Education, Teachers College, Columbia University.

Gordon, E.W., Bridglall, B.L. & Meroe, A.S. (2005). *Supplementary education: The hidden curriculum of high academic achievement*. Latham, MD: Rowan and Littlefield.

Heath, S. B. (2000). Making learning work. *Afterschool Matters: Dialogues in Philosophy, Practice and Evaluation, 1(1)*, 33-45.

Heath, S. B., Soep, E. & Roach, A. (1998). Living the arts through language and learning: A report on community-based youth organizations. *Americans for the Arts Monographs* 2(7),1-20.

Holzman, L. (1997). *Schools for growth: Radical alternatives to current educational models.* Mahwah, NJ: Erlbaum.

Holzman, L. (2002). *Young people learn by studying themselves: The All Stars Talent Show in action.* NY: East Side Institute for Short Term Psychotherapy. DVD.

Holzman, L. (2006). Activating postmodernism. *Theory & Psychology, 16(1)*, 109-123.

Holzman, L. (2009). *Vygotsky at work and play.* New York and London: Routledge.

Lantoff, J. P. (Ed), (2000). *Sociocultural theory and second language learning.* Oxford: Oxford University Press.

Lidz, C.S. & Gindis, B. (2003). Dynamic assessment of the evolving cognitive functions in children. In A. Kozulin, B. Gindis, V.S. Ageyev, & S.M. Miller (Eds.), *Vygotsky's Educational Theory In Cultural Context,* (pp. 99-116). New York: Cambridge University Press.

MacNaughton, G. & Williams, G. (1998). *Techniques for teaching young children: Choices in theory and practice.* French Forests, Australia: Longman.

Mahoney, J.L., Larson, R.W. & Eccles, J.S. (2005). (Eds.). *Organized activities as contexts of development: Extracurricular activities, after school and community programs.* Mahwah, NJ: Erlbaum.

Newman, F. & Holzman, L. (1993). *Lev Vygotsky: Revolutionary scientist.* London: Routledge.

Newman, F. & Holzman, L (1997). *The end of knowing: A new developmental way of learning.* London: Routledge.

Newman, D. Griffin, P. & Cole, M. (1989). *The construction zone: Working for cognitive change in school.* Cambridge: Cambridge University Press.

Nicolopoulou, A., & Cole, M. (1993). The generation and transmission of shared knowledge in the culture of collaborative learning: The Fifth Dimension, its play world, and its institutional contexts. In E. A. Forman, N. Minick, and C. A. Stone (Eds.), *Contexts for learning: Sociocultural dynamics in children's development* (pp. 283-314). New York: Oxford University Press.

Rodgers, A. & Rodgers, E. M. (2004). *Scaffolding literacy instruction. Strategies for K-4 classrooms.* Portsmouth, NH: Heinemann.

Rogoff, B. (1990). *Apprenticeship in thinking: Cognitive development in social context.* New York: Oxford University Press.

Rogoff, B. & Lave, J. (1984). (Eds.), *Everyday cognition: Development in social context* (pp. 95-117). Boston: Harvard University Press.

Shotter, J. (1989). Vygotsky's psychology: Joint activity in the zone of proximal development. *New Ideas in Psychology, 7,* 185-204.

Tharp, R. G. & Gallimore, R. (1988). *Rousing minds to life: Teaching, learning and schooling in social context.* Cambridge, England: Cambridge University Press.

Vygotsky, L.S. (1978). *Mind in society.* Cambridge, MA: Harvard University Press.

Vygotsky, L. S. (1987). *The collected works of L. S. Vygotsky. Vol. 1.* New York: Plenum.

Vygotsky, L.S. (1994). The problem of the environment. In R. van der Veer & J. Valsiner (Eds.), *The Vygotsky reader* (pp. 338-354). Oxford: Blackwell.

Vygotsky, L.S. (1997). The historical meaning of the crisis in psychology: A methodological investigation. In *The collected works of L.S.Vygotsky, Volume 3* (pp. 233-343). New York: Plenum.

Vygotsky, L.S. (2004). The collective as a factor in the development of the abnormal child. In R.W. Rieber and D. K. Robinson (Eds.), *The essential Vygotsky* (pp. 201-219). NY: Kluwer Academic/Plenum Publishers.

Wertsch, J. V. (1985). *Vygotsky and the social formation of mind.* Cambridge, MA: Harvard University Press.

Wertsch, J.V. (1991). *Voices of the mind: A sociolcultural approach to mediated action.* Cambridge MA: Harvard University Press.

Wood, D., Bruner, J. & Ross, G. (1976). The role of tutoring in problem-solving. *Journal of Child Psychology and Psychiatry, 17,* 89-100.

Notes

1 Vygotsky used the Russian word "obuchenie," which refer to both teaching and learning. It is usually translated as "learning."

2 Lantolf and Thorne (2006) note this misunderstanding and make a worthwhile distinction between scaffolding and development in the ZPD.

3 What I am describing as completion would be identified in language acquisition and linguistics literature by other terms, such as expansion or contingency, which are located within a cognitive framework. My expansion/liberal interpretation of Vygotsky's terms is not.

4 Reports on the advantages of culturally-based outside-of-school programs, including arguments that they can help close "the achievement gap" are many. See for example, Arts Education Partnership, 1999; Bodilly and Beckett, 2005; Carnegie Council on Adolescent Development, 1992; Childress, 1998; Heath, 2000; Heath, Soep and Roach, 1998; Gordon, Bridglall and Meroe, 2005; and Mahoney, Larson and Eccles, 2005.

Big Ideas and Revolutionary Activity

Power, Authority and Pointless Activity

Fred Newman and Lois Holzman

Power, Authority, and Pointless Activity (The Developmental Discourse of Social Therapy) discusses our understanding of, and our relationship to, power. For Newman and Holzman, the socio-political description is easiest to understand when viewed as a "dialectical relationship to authority." In our current socio-political situation, power and authority are often thought of as synonymous, yet this is far from the truth. Authority imposes power from the top down, yet, power can also be created and expressed from the bottom up. Social therapy takes on the activity of eliminating the authoritarian structure of power by shifting our focus to the collective creation of it. By exploring this paradox, the group performs therapy together and creates new ways of relating, engaging and growing. A synthesis of Vygotskian, Marxian and Wittgensteinian assertions about language, dialectics and performance, social therapy groups engage in the activity of talk, not the substance or pragmatic functions of it, creating their own language and discovering not truths, but the power of collectively creating meaning.

If excitement about postmodern and discursive therapies has recently waned, as editors Tom Strong and David Pare suggest, perhaps this is because, for the most part, these therapies are all talk! This is, paradoxically, their strength relative to mainstream modernist therapies and their limitation relative to what is needed if we human beings are to transform our emotionality so as to prevent our killing ourselves off (whether quickly or painfully slowly).

We have been asked to speak concretely and practically to readers, to show our therapeutic approach—social therapy—in action, to stay grounded in our practice—and we will. However, we must, as well, situate ourselves as "on the left" of the postmodern spectrum, both methodologically and politically—which, we hope to show, is neither a characteristic nor the "location" of social therapy, but its activity. To do so, we need to speak to the issue of power.

Power and Authority Revisited

Among the more thoughtful Marxist critiques of postmodernism is Ian Parker's "Against Postmodernism: Psychology in Cultural Context," which appeared in *Theory & Psychology* (Parker, 1998). Parker's critique of postmodernism is, as we understand it, valid. What is his criticism? Essentially, that most versions of postmodernism avoid or deny the issue or question of *power*. Parker has leveled this attack against postmodernism in general and, we must add in the name of intellectual honesty, at virtually all of our positive writings on postmodernism. Some postmodernists avoid

Big Ideas and Revolutionary Activity

the issue (question, topic, etc). of power, we imagine, because they take power to be the fundamental flaw of modernism and, therefore, it is precisely what postmodernism must get rid of (as if avoiding something gets rid of it!). Others, with varying degrees of sophistication, deconstruct and discard power as a necessary component of social life. We have always been somewhat bewildered by Parker's critique of our efforts since we regard all that we have written—and far more importantly, what we have organized or created—as a postmodern explication/expression of power. For we believe that the matter of power (not to mention the power of matter) must be postmodernized if we are to go beyond postmodernism as a mere stage of modernism (Jameson, 1984).

Power (or the word "power" if you prefer), no doubt, has multiple meanings. But, as we have long argued, the socio-political sense of power is best understood in its dialectical relationship to *authority*. First, some simpleminded remarks. Authority goes from the top, down. It is imposed. Most importantly, it must be known. Power comes from the bottom, up. It is expressed. It is created. Obviously, in ordinary language, power and authority are often treated as synonymous. Yet nothing could be further from the truth (in our view, everything is equidistant from the truth, viz. an infinite distance!). But the commonplace confusion of the two, power and authority, says a great deal about the *authoritarian* structure of our ontic, now worldwide, culture. For not only are commodities fetishized—turned into god-like authorities, a la Marx—but *everything* is commodified. Hence knowledge, scientific and otherwise, is God-like here in late-modernism/early postmodernism.

The fetishization of knowledge has led some philosophers (for example, Newman, 1999; Newman and Holzman, 1996 ; Rorty, 1982, 2000) to abandon it, and others (for example, Davidson, 2000) to attempt to rehabilitate it. But even "getting rid" of knowledge is not enough. The more serious issue (activity) is eliminating the *authority of knowledge* in favor of the *creativity of power*—not to mention the power of creativity. Even Davidson, the supreme rehabilitator, recognizes the defect of knowing as an authoritarian conception. He believes we can overcome that defect analytically, i.e. philosophically, and he is no doubt right (he almost always is!). But it would make no difference, since philosophy (analytical or otherwise) has for many years now had little or nothing to do with the activities and the struggles of ordinary people. Philosophy has no one to blame for that except contemporary philosophers. Newman and Rorty have not abandoned philosophy. Rather, they are unwilling to abandon people in the name of the ever-shrinking academic niche into which philosophy has retreated. Unless postmodernism wishes to become as irrelevant as institutionalized philosophy, it must move beyond a *deconstruction* of knowing (which, in its extreme form, is an *elimination* of knowing, Newman & Holzman, 1997) to an active reconstruction of power—*the activity of power*.

In its historic roots (religious, legal, scientific, civic, etc). authority is dominantly individualistic. The "author" is, for the most part, an individual, an actor, an agent. There is, strictly speaking, no activity of authority. It is fundamentally *regulatory*.

Authority is an inactive negative for essentially inhibiting growth and development in the name of those in control—or, as we sometimes confusedly say, in the name of those "in power." But being "in power" (somewhat ironically) does not at all involve the activity of power. It is, rather, the commodification of power (labor power) into authority. And while commodities can be sold, they do not develop; they are consumed. Authority stifles growth. It is not a necessary evil. It is an unnecessary evil. What is necessary for development is the activity of power, the exercise of power, the development of power by the many—collectively, democratically and creatively. It is the work of the laborer, Marx teaches us, that creates value (Marx, 1967). It is the authoritarian commodification of this process that yields a *realization* of this value which, in turn, maintains the authority of the owners of the means of production.

But authority (vs. power) goes well beyond the economic sphere. It is constantly present, under capitalism, in the psychological sphere. The human capacity to authoritarianly commodify oneself is in constant psychological struggle with the human desire and capacity to exercise power *without commodification*, i.e., freely. This understanding, first articulated by one of us in a vulgarly ultra-left political form in *Power and Authority* (Newman, 1974), has been refined in practice, over decades, into what is now identified as *social therapy*.

Our efforts to give meaning to the concept of power led us to practicing and speaking of the *activity* of power rather than either a *definition* of power (a classical modernist mistake) or the *use* of power (a revisionist understanding of Wittgenstein). In our view, a careful and sympathetic reading of Wittgenstein (such as that of Baker, 1992) suggests that it is not meaning and use which are equatable, but meaning and the *activity of using*. Meaning is a *doing*, not an interpretation. ("the *speaking* of language is part of an activity, or of a form of life," Wittgenstein, 1953, p. 11). The use of something, on the other hand, is a functional interpretation (an Aristotelian essence)—What is a chair used for? To sit on? The activity of using is, in point of fact, what the chair *is* used for (standing on it to swat a mosquito). The meaning of a term is not its interpretive use but what it is (*in activity*) used for. Wittgenstein's "slab" examples (Wittgenstein, 1953) make this point precisely because the function of the "slab" is unknown (indeed, unknowable). The endless "ordinary language" analyses, based presumably on Wittgenstein's later writings, bear little or no resemblance to the pointlessness of Wittgenstein's "slab" examples—indeed, to the pointlessness of all of Wittgenstein's later thinking. Thus, it is the activity of power, not the pointedness of power, that interests us in social therapy and, indeed, throughout our organized postmodernist community.

Postmodernism must be an organized activity—it must be performed—if it is to be truly powerful. The temptation to keep postmodernism unorganized, or even disorganized, is a misunderstood libertarianism, an anti-power perspective—ultimately, a liberal authoritarian perspective. Postmodernism must reorganize the world in anti-authoritarian ways, i.e. in *power*ful ways. But powerful ways must be activities. As with Aristotle's practical syllogism, "the conclusion" of postmodernist understanding

Big Ideas and Revolutionary Activity

must be an action (more precisely, an activity). For postmodernist understanding is a moral discourse. It goes from descriptive premises to a normative activist conclusion (in Aristotle's language, an action). It is not a mode of thought going from description (interpretation) to description (interpretation). It is a journey from "what is" to "what ought to be." As such, it is creative and powerful.

While Aristotle's remarks about the practical syllogism (his ethics) are an interesting prefiguration of our activist manifesto, Aristotle was, of course, the grandfather of dualism. And modernism is, arguably, little more than dualism writ large. From Lovejoy to Dewey to Quine to Davidson to Rorty, and on and on and on, dualism has been under attack for a century. Still, it flourishes, largely because, as we noted earlier, philosophy (including critical philosophy) is so alienated from the popular culture. Postmodernism's efforts to present a critique of deadly dualism in a more popular voice has brought nasty self-serving criticism from the establishment intellectual community—including, of course, the philosophers. In their efforts to defend themselves from these vicious pseudo-intellectual attacks, postmodernists have for the most part noticeably avoided the theoretical psychological writings of Lev Vygotsky, no doubt because he was a Marxist—and a Soviet Marxist at that. But, in our view, Vygotsky's critique of psychological dualism is potentially of great value in understanding the activity of power and the creation of a new psychology.

First, Vygotsky gave us a new conception of method, one that is not dualistically instrumental—tool for result—but monistically dialectical—*method as simultaneously tool-and-result* (Vygotsky, 1978, p. 65).[1] With this, the scientific community could have finally ended the theory-practice debate, yet still it persists, even among postmodernists. Second, his *zone of proximal development* offered psychology a way out of the conundrums generated by its dualistic framework: person-environment, self-other, internal-external, to name the most longstanding (Vygotsky, 1978). As we understand Vygotsky, learning and development in early childhood is a tool-and-result activity in which learning leads—dialectically, not linearly—development, a phenomenon made possible by the social, collective construction of the environment that makes learning-and-development possible (Newman & Holzman, 1993). Creating zones of proximal development is the activity of power.

Third, Vygotsky deconstructed the centuries-old dualism between thought and word and, in so doing, he provided a means for the rejection of not only the pictorial but also the pragmatic view of language. His position can be seen in the following remarks:

> The relationship of thought to word is not a thing but a process, a movement from thought to word and from word to thought ... Thought is not expressed but completed in the word. We can, therefore, speak of the establishment (i.e., the unity of being and nonbeing) of thought in the word. Any thought strives to unify, to establish a relationship between one thing and another. Any thought has movement. It unfolds. (1987, p. 250)

> The structure of speech is not simply the mirror image of the structure of thought. It cannot, therefore, be placed on thought like clothes off a rack. Speech does not merely serve as the expression of developed thought.
>
> Thought is restructured as it is transformed into speech. It is not expressed but completed in the word. Therefore, precisely because of the contrasting directions of movement, the development of the internal and external aspects of speech forms a true unity. (1987, p. 251)

There are not two separate worlds, the private one of thinking and the social one of speaking. There is, instead, the dialectical unity, speaking/thinking. Children would not be able to perform as speakers, and thereby learn to speak, if thinking/speaking were not a *completive social activity*. Like Wittgenstein, Vygotsky provided the basis for a non-dualistic (non-expressionist, non-descriptive) conception of language and a method for moving beyond epistemology (even a social one) to a new ontology of activity.

Social therapeutic practice is in many ways a synthesis of Wittgenstein's and Vygotsky's approach to language and human subjectivity (Newman & Holzman, 1996, 1997). "Completion" is far more than a critique of dualism. It is a positive (postmodern) move (an activist move) beyond dualism. It is not, like dualism, secretly value laden. It is not pointed. It is (like Wittgenstein) properly pointless. As such, it is a useful frame of reference for a value-free psychology—indeed, for an infinitude of value-free psychologies. Creating these psychologies—actively creating new psychologies—is, in our view, the critical work (the revolutionary activity) of postmodernism.

Social therapy—Pointless, Powerful and Paradoxical

If you have been following our argument, you may have spotted some seeming paradoxes. Two are of particular relevance to the doing of social therapy. One, if individuals have become commodified selves, how can they exercise their power freely, i.e., uncommodified? Two, we seem to be saying that morality and moral discourse can and ought to be pointless and value free, but aren't these the very things that comprise morality and moral discourse? We will take each of these in turn.

Typically, people come into therapy groups, as they come into any group setting, individuated. They want help and think that the way to get it is individualistically— a perfectly understandable notion, given that in our culture people are socialized to an individuated learning and development model. They say things like, "I had this awful fight with my mother last night. I was furious....and I'm really upset right now." They look to the therapist for some advice, solution, interpretation, explanation or, in more postmodern approaches, leadership in a collaborative process that might generate some new understanding of themselves. They are, again understandably, appealing to *authority*—that of the therapist, of knowledge and of language. To the extent that *power* is a relevant concern to them, they want only to "feel more powerful," by which they typically mean that they want, *as individuals*, to have "more control" over their lives.

Big Ideas and Revolutionary Activity

People come to social therapy with similar understandings and expectations, even if they might have heard that it isn't like "ordinary" therapy. Social therapy is not designed to help individuals with their individual problems, nor to help individuals feel or become more powerful, since we believe that only authority—and not power—is ascribable to individuals. It is, rather, designed to help people *exercise* their collective power to create new emotional growth, a process that requires deconstructing the sense of self (an authoritarian commodification) and reconstructing the concept of social relationship.

Our experience is that this comes, not from some abstract ideological commitment, but from a participatory process in which people actually construct something together— namely, the group. The key focus in social therapy is building the group. Groups are typically composed of 10-25 people, a mix of women and men of varying ages, ethnicities, sexual orientations, professions and "problems." Most groups are ongoing (although we do some time-limited groups) and meet weekly for 90 minutes. Members' length of time in group varies; some people remain for years, others for shorter periods of time, and new members join periodically.

Power is the creative capacity of the group—by the exercise of its emotional labor—to generate new environments; authority is the societally overdetermined predisposition of the individuated members of the group to passively accept class-dominated, patriarchal emotive environments. Conflict between the two gets played out in social therapy groups, where the unit of transformation/change/growth/learning is the group, and the therapist is simultaneously the organizer of the group's emotive labor power and the potential (or even actual) repository of the group members' "authoritarian instincts." The ongoing process of social therapy is the working out of this relationship; as the group engages in the activity of building the group, it is changing its relationship to power and to authority and becoming more powerful. As one social therapy group member, a man in his early 40s, put it: "The social therapy term 'building the group' is probably the one that drives people crazy more than any other. It's so hard to get your head around! There's a vagueness and a clarity about it at the same time. It's what's going on in group. Early on, you can't see it even though you know something's happening."[2]

In this process people come to appreciate what—and that—they can create. Simultaneously, they come to realize the limitations of trying to learn, grow and create individually and that growth comes from participating in the process of building the groups in which one functions. This new learning rekindles development—development by virtue of the group growing. In social therapeutic terms, human development is the activity of creating the conditions for development (Vygotsky's zone of proximal development) and the unit that engages in this activity is the group (the collective).

A recent social therapy group began with a woman, very upset, asking for help. She described what was going on at her job as a teacher in an inner-city school, things she and the group members found oppressive and oppressing. Some members of the group responded that they would like to help but that how she was asking was all about herself and her problem and wasn't connected to them or to the work the group had been doing for weeks. The woman acknowledged various group members' comments, but persisted in being upset and saying she needed help with this problem. At one point, she turned to the therapist and asked him for help. He suggested that she respond to the group. She kept pursuing her agenda and group members were becoming exasperated. One long-time member of the group burst into an impassioned and very moving "speech" about how she too comes to group wanting to be taken care of, given advice, etc. for what's going on with her, but she never gets it. Instead, she said, the therapist insists that help comes from building the group, the struggle over that ensues, people do some building, and she leaves group every week feeling very loved and helped from the work.

Then a woman new to the group said that she knew she couldn't get help with her personal problems in social therapy, but that this was OK with her. One or two group members—including the upset woman who had begun the group and had been its focus for much of the time—supported her, others disagreed, and the group went around on this topic for a while. The therapist then said that as he understood it, those who believed that social therapy doesn't deal with people's personal problems had a misunderstanding. Indeed, it does—*building the group* is how social therapy helps people with their personal problems. He contrasted how people go to therapy with how they go to a medical doctor. You might go to a medical doctor for a pain in your eye, he said, but if after some conversation and examination, he tells you he has to treat your kidney, you might be surprised but you probably won't fight with him and insist that he must help you in "your way." The social conventions of medicine and illness and health are such that we accept the doctor's way of helping us. But therapy, evidently, is a different story. People come to therapy not only with their personal problems, but also committed to a particular way of getting help with them. The group then worked with another group member who wanted help with problems he was having dealing with his young son; they experimented and played with ways of talking (asking for help) so as to contribute to the growth of the group.

This particular social therapy group session highlights—in both form and substance—the group's active struggle with its power (of collective creativity) and authority (of individual knowing). It also suggests the activistic and collective way that the social therapist responds to therapy talk. She or he conveys, in varying ways, that what is being said ("I had a fight; I'm upset; I need help") is of no interest (qua social therapy) except in so far as the group can make use of it in the activity of creating itself into a new socialized helping environment, i.e., in its exercise of power. The task of the group is to *do* something with what people say in therapy, something that contributes to the social process of development. The social therapist works with the group (not the individuated selves that, reductionistically speaking, comprise the group) to organize itself to engage in this process of building the group. In this process the group becomes an *emotional zone of proximal development (emotional zpd)*. The various

Big Ideas and Revolutionary Activity

members, each at different levels of emotional development, are encouraged to create a new unit with a new level of emotional development, i.e., the group's level of emotional development. This process involves a qualitative change of therapeutic focus—from the individuated self who discovers deeper insights into his or her consciousness to the collective engaged in the continuous activity of creating a new social unit, the emotional zpd. The overriding question transforms from "How is each individual doing?" to "How well is the group performing its activity?" A longtime social therapy group member speaks to how this impacts: "The focus in social therapy on the group and not the individual is really helpful. It helps you get out of yourself. It changes your orientation to the world, how things are organized in the world."

Social therapy's ultra-focus on activity, specifically on the activity of speaking, i.e., on the conversation, transforms meaning itself. Reconsidering Wittgenstein from a Marxian and Vygotskian activity-theoretic vantage point, social therapy rejects the equation of meaning and use that is common among many followers and students of Wittgenstein in favor of the dialectical relationship between meaning and activity. Meaning is created, Vygotsky has shown, through the activity of speaking completing thinking. Social therapy extends ("completes") Vygotsky's picture in the following manner. If thinking-speaking is a continuous process of completing, then the "completer" need not be the same person who is doing the thinking. *Others can complete for us.* When people speak, participate in a dialogue, discussion or conversation (or write), we are not simply *saying* what's going on but are *creating* what's going on. And we understand each other by virtue of engaging in this shared creative activity. As one newcomer to social therapy commented, "Social therapy is like a new practice of relationship. In our group the creating of our conversation is the activity of our interconnectedness."

Inevitably, and nearly continuously, the group confronts the conflict between our socio-culturally constructed adherence to authority and our world-historic capacity to exercise power, as we saw in the group session discussed above. *"How can we talk so that our talking helps build the group?"* This question encapsulates the group's process of discovering a method of relating to talk relationally rather than individualistically—in Wittgenstein's terms, as "activity, or a form of life;" in Vygotsky's terms, "completively" not expressively. It is the activity of talk—not the substance of talk (its aboutness) nor the use of talk (its societal pragmatic function)—that is the focus of the group's activity. The authority of language (as expressive of truth, reality and self) is challenged explicitly as people falteringly attempt to converse in this new way, to create meaning together. Commenting on her group, one woman said, "The group creates a different language in the course of a group [session]. I never realized that the meaning of words is so contextualized. We create a vocabulary and a language that's particular to each group."

In this process, group members come to see that what they are saying to each other has no meaning other than what they create. Like poets, they become meaning makers, creators of language and of a new conception of language, one that is non-essentialist and non-descriptive. It is in the creating of their poem, the therapeutic conversation, that the group exercises its power.

A woman began a recent group saying that she still hated her father. She couldn't be absolutely sure, but she thought he was always out to abuse her, he looked at her in a certain way, etc. The initial response of several group members—a line of questioning that is typical in this kind of situation—was to ask for details (what happened, when, for how long, etc). in order to find out what "really" happened, was she "really" abused, etc.— that is, in order to get to the "truth." After about twenty minutes, the group began to question what this woman meant by some of the words she was saying and how it was that she was saying them ("What do you mean when you say 'you hate him'; what do you mean by 'abuse'; why are you saying this to us now," etc.), and these words and their contextualization (the group's *doing* of meaning) became the focus of the conversation.

At this point, the group had abandoned the pursuit of truth in favor of exploring the activity of their speaking together. This changed activity—from trying to find the truth to creating meanings—created a group sense of new meaning rather than a collective sense of truth. Engaging in this activity, the group gains a heightened understanding that finding truth is not possible, that meanings are created collectively and that they have the power to create meanings. In the words of one group member, "The challenge in our group is always to not take what's said as truth. We don't always succeed! It's very freeing, though, when I can hear and see what so-and-so is saying and doing and not experience it as 'This is really what they're doing and so this is what I have to do in response.' People say words and we don't know what they mean until we create their meaning. The group grows a lot by taking ownership of what it creates."

All we have said thus far relates to the question of the place of morality in postmodernism in general and postmodern therapies in particular. Morality as we know it is authoritarian—it comes from the top, it is imposed, and it must be known. Certain behaviors, acts, values and beliefs are wrenched out of the ongoing life process and reified into a code or system of conduct. People (or peoples) are then judged by how well they conform to the code or system. Moral discourse is always in reference to authority (the knower or the known, a god, truth, dogma, belief, system or rule, etc.). In trying to escape authoritarianism, much of postmodernism accepts or embraces alternative moralities (i.e., codes or systems of conduct). For this, it is accused by some of being "rampantly relativist" and/or amoral (Parker, 1998; Rosenau, 1992). And we agree that it is, so long as it fails to reject the ontological premise of modernist morality. Why it hasn't is unclear to us, for there surely is no evidence that human beings require a moral system in order to know what to do. Throughout history, countless terrible things have been done in the name of moral systems (and people seem no better able to know what to do for having such a system). Human beings no more need a code of ethics in order to live morally than children need rules of grammar in order to speak. Neither activity requires an *appeal* to any authority. It is

Big Ideas and Revolutionary Activity

human activity that produces both.

With activity as the ontological unit of human life, social therapy rejects morality (an authoritarian code or system) in favor of *moral activity*. Ordinary people create morality in ordinary ways every day. When it is not commodified into a finished product or code (and then imposed on its creators by others, usually those "in power"), but is allowed to be continuously created and developed by its creators, then moral activity is another tool-and-result of the social process of making meaning. It is then not authoritarian but powerful.

Sharing his experience in social therapy, a man in his early 30s brought up the topic of morality: "There's a certain morality to social therapy. It's not so judgmental, not into 'people should be a certain way.' It opens up space for people to be *all* the ways they are. The question is what people do together, not how they are. I'm much closer to people now. It used to be that my relationships were based on what people said five minutes ago or five months ago. But that keeps you distant. In group, we're freed up to have certain kinds of dialogues not based on your interpretation of what people say or on how you're feeling or how they're feeling. It challenges us to be open to bringing something into the mix so we can constantly create something."

In so far as it is realizable, human freedom lies in our collective ability to create meaning, not in our individualistic capacity to discern truth. In social therapy we "make the problems vanish" (following Wittgenstein, 1980) by changing their meaning through an appeal to the collective capacity, responsibility and creative power of the group.

And why isn't all of this just a vulgar idealism? Because, in practice, the philosophically religious dualism, Realist-Idealist, is rejected in favor of an activity-theoretic *world* (more accurately, *life*) view. Social therapy is a humanistic radical rejection of all forms of reductionism. This leaves us with only one tool to build with: human activity. And that tool is a tool-and-result. The anthropological discovery of humans as tool users was the theoretical basis of humanistic Marxism. The psychological discovery of moral humans as tool-and-result users is the theoretical basis of humanistic postmodern Marxism. All creative power to the activity of the people!

References

Brandom, R. B. (Ed). (2000). *Rorty and his critics*. Oxford: Blackwell.

Davidson, D. (2000). Truth rehabilitated. In R. B. Brandom (Ed.), *Rorty and his critics*. Oxford: Blackwell.

Jameson, F. (1984). Postmodernism, or the cultural logic of late capitalism. *New Left Review, 146*, 53-93.

Marx, K. (1967). *Capital* (Volume 1). New York: International Publishers.

Newman, F. (1999). One dogma of dialectical materialism. *Annual Review of Critical Psychology, 1*, 83-99.

Newman, F. (1974). *Power and authority: The inside view of class struggle.* New York: Centers for Change.

Newman, F. & Holzman, L. (1993). *Lev Vygotsky: Revolutionary scientist.* London: Routledge.

Newman, F. & Holzman, L. (1996). *Unscientific psychology: A cultural-performatory approach to understanding human life.* Westport, CT: Praeger.

Newman, F. & Holzman, L. (1997). *The end of knowing: A new developmental way of learning.* London: Routledge.

Parker, I. (1998). Against postmodernism: Psychology in cultural context. *Theory & Psychology, 8*(5), 621-647.

Rorty, R. (2000). Universality and truth. In R. B. Brandom (Ed.), *Rorty and his critics.* Oxford: Blackwell.

Rosenau, P.M. (1992). *Post-modernism and the social sciences: Insights, inroads and intrusions.* Princeton, NJ: Princeton University Press.

Vygotsky, L.S. (1978). *Mind in society.* Cambridge, MA: Harvard University Press.

Vygotsky, L. S. (1987). *The collected works of L. S. Vygotsky. Vol. 1.* New York: Plenum.

Wittgenstein, L. (1953). *Philosophical investigations.* Oxford: Basil Blackwell.

Wittgenstein, L (1980). *Remarks on the philosophy of psychology.* Oxford: Blackwell.

Footnotes

[1] The search for method becomes one of the most important problems of the entire enterprise of understanding the uniquely human forms of psychological activity. In this case, the method is simultaneously prerequisite and product, the tool and the result of the study (Vygotsky, 1978, p. 65).

[2] This and subsequent quotations from social therapy clients are taken from an ongoing interview project.

Big Ideas and Revolutionary Activity

Invited Talks

Big Ideas and Revolutionary Activity

Creating Communities of Hope

Keynote Lecture

*2016 International Conference of Allies Across Boundaries:
Diverse Practices of Education and Human Potential Development
National Dong-Hwa University, Hualien Taiwan November 18-19, 2016*

Creating Communities of Hope discusses Lois's dedication to the study and practice of play and performance, advocating their role in collective (re)creation, learning and development. Her extensive background as an activist and a play revolutionary has provided her with keen insights on the extraordinary ability of play and performance to qualitatively transform communities. Recognizing that our society is suffering from an ever-growing gap between our developmental needs and our learning needs, Lois indicates that the way we understand and practice learning is misguided due to the way it separates learning and play from development. Lois also critiques psychology and the way it hinders our development by treating people as products, perpetuating ideals like "normalcy," which leads to "othering." In contrast, by embracing an activity-based, inter-relational methodology, Lois's new psychology invites us to become active reshapers of our environments--creators of growth, learning, community and emotionality—asserting that play and performance are the keys to revolutionizing our currently stagnant (and traumatized) society.

I speak to you today about education as a revolutionary and as a play revolutionary. A revolutionary because I've chosen to live my life as an activist who uses my academic background and experience to organize people—as individuals and communities—to participate in creating their development. A play revolutionary because I have seen first-hand in hundreds and hundreds of cases the power of play to reinitiate development and learning, to allow people to see new possibilities, to create new ways of being in the world with themselves and others, and to generate hope. And whether we think that these are or should be the goals of education, we know that we are living in a time when education is incapable of meeting these goals. I will share with you how it is that education cannot succeed in the absence of play. But I will not stop there, for that would be quite depressing. I'll also share a new understanding of play and its relationship to learning and development, give some examples of successful practices, and perhaps inspire hope.

Certainly, in the US—and from what I can see and have been told—in most nations, we are suffering from a growing gap between our development needs and our learning needs.

This gap stems in large part from how learning has come to be understood and practiced. Educational institutions are structured and function with a misguided

Big Ideas and Revolutionary Activity

conception of learning, misguided because it separates learning from development and from play and takes learning to be the acquisition of skills and information. The acquisition of skills and information is the assimilation of what already exists. And while this is of course necessary for adaptation to a society and culture, it does not lead to qualitative transformation, growth of individuals or communities, or new possibilities for a society, culture or the world. For that, we need development. Development is the creating of something new. You can learn a particular thing acquisitionally, but you can only become a learner if you learn developmentally. Becoming a learner requires the transformation of who you are, not an accumulation of what you know. Without the continuous development of people, our societies may prove incapable of producing *learners*.

Similar to a misconception of learning, educational institutions operate with a misguided conception of human development. This conception comes from the dominant Western psychology, which permeates the world. It says that human development happens *to* individuals; it says human development is an evolutionary, hierarchical and essentially internal process. It says that human development takes place in a sequence of stages. And it says that first you reach a developmental stage and then you learn.

This is the psychology of development I was trained in and that I reject. I reject it because in my experience that's not how people grow. I reject it because it does not foster the development of people, but, in fact, it hinders it. It is all about people as products and not as active producers. It has a politic of maintaining the status quo. Its methods and conceptions glorify individualism and stifle collective action. It holds up science and reason as humanity's saviors and denigrates art and creativity. And in doing all this, psychology contributes to educational failure.

So, 40 years ago I began—with wonderful colleagues—to create a new psychology, one that we call a psychology of becoming and social therapeutics.

This new psychology has a different starting point from what we know as psychology. Instead of positing the individual as primary, as what human beings are, its starting point is relationality. We are social beings—first, last and everyplace in between. Instead of seeing growth and development as something that happens *to* us, from inside out, in the new psychology, we *create* our development and growth. Instead of being about who people are and how they tick compared to some norms psychology made up, the new psychology sees human beings as simultaneously who we are and other than who we are, or who we are becoming. Instead of seeing human beings as only shaped by environment, in the new psychology human beings also reshape and create our environments.

The method of this new psychology is to organize all kinds of people—young and old, rich, poor and in-between—to become active reshapers of their environments. Creators of their emotionality, their learning, their growth, their communities. It's an activity that re-initiates hope and imagination—allowing us to see new possibilities and make them happen. Within education, then, if you want all students to become successful learners, then you and they together must transform the environments in which they are not successful learners. That's the developmental activity needed to develop learners. That's developmental learning.

Here is where play comes in. When we play, learning and development are inseparable. Play is how we learn developmentally. Play is how we become learners. Just look at babies.

They learn-play seamlessly and continuously all day long.

They play with everyone and everything.

We're all here because we played our way into becoming who we are today. Way back when, we were babbling, crawling little babies. Way back when, we played—and it changed everything. We played at speaking and walking before we knew how to speak or walk, and that's how come we became speakers and walkers. Our caregivers helped us (they played right along with us) and they absolutely loved us for it and cheered us on. They helped us play at being "bigger" and older and more skilled than we actually were —or as one of my heroes, the early 20th century psychologist Lev Vygotsky, says— as if we are "a head taller" than we are.

> "In play a child always behaves beyond his average age, above his daily behavior; in play it is as though he were ***a head taller*** than himself.
>
> In this sense, play is a major source of development."
>
> *Lev Vygotsky*

This phrase—a head taller—captures how and why human beings develop and learn— because we are not only who are at any given moment or age or stage of life. We are also other than who we are. **We are simultaneously who we are AND who we are becoming.** We are babies who can't speak a language AND—through play— we are speakers.

In Play, We...
- Go beyond ourselves
- Do things without knowing how
- Relate as who we are and who we're becoming—at the very same time
- Create something new out of what exists

Big Ideas and Revolutionary Activity

It turns out there's another human activity with the same characteristics as play. In English we call it performance, like what actors do on the stage. Like babies, actors get to be both who they are AND someone other than who they are (their character) AT THE SAME TIME.

As with play, when we perform we go beyond ourselves and do things without knowing how. We relate as who we are and other than who we are. We create something new out of what exists.

This playful and performatory way of being in the world with others is something that all of us, at any age, can do. But most of us stop. It's not our fault. A bias against play is deep in our culture. We're taught that play is frivolous. That there's a difference between learning and playing—and that learning is what matters. We're told that performance is being phony or fake—and that being "your true self'" is what's important. We're told constantly who we are—and that limits who we can become. We focus on getting it right and looking good—and that stops us from developing. Without play, we get stuck. Without performing in new ways, we get stuck. Individuals get stuck. Families get stuck. Communities get stuck. Nations get stuck. Indeed, these days the whole world appears stuck in old roles, stale performances, destructive games, and emotional turmoil.

Being stuck is standing still. To get unstuck, we have to move. And play is MOVEMENT. Performance is MOVEMENT. In physical space, in time, **and in the always becoming-ness of our lives**. When we move, we get a new perspective. Turn your head 90 degrees and what you see is different from what you saw seconds ago. Walk your usual route to work or home as a tourist there for the very first time and you'll have a new perspective. Strike a power pose as you walk into a meeting with your boss or professor and you'll feel different about the conversation you're about to have.

When we play and perform, we move about and around what's there in our surroundings and in how we feel, see and experience. We can see old things in new ways and we can see new things, things we've never seen before. Walk into your house or dorm room backwards and you'll see it in a new way. Try dancing with your brother or sister or roommate when you get home instead of mumbling hello. We discover what's always been there. We create new ways to feel, new ideas and new beliefs. We discover AND create what we're made of.

Helping people move around old ways of being and seeing and doing and feeling is what my colleagues and I do. We support them to be active participants in creating their and their community's learning and development—continuously. We call our practice social therapeutics as a new psychology of becoming.

Selected Essays, Talks and Articles by Lois Holzman

Social Therapeutics: A Psychology of Becoming

Social Therapeutics is an approach to human development, community development and social change that relates to people of all ages and life circumstances as social performers and creators of their lives and culture

Our work is realized, manifested and developed through a network of independent organizations that we have built and expanded over 40 years. Two guiding principles were there at the start and remain to this day.

First, to be independently funded and supported, and not take money or be constrained by government, corporate, university, foundation or other traditional funding sources. This involved reaching out to ordinary Americans for financial support and participation, by stopping them on street corners and knocking on the doors of their homes. That activity allowed individuals to become active participants in the activities and organizations we were building together—citizens in the best sense of that word. And because we reached out to all sorts of people on the streets and by knocking at their doors, what has evolved is a new kind of partnership between wealthy and middle class Americans and the poor, a partnership that sidesteps the institutions and assumptions of tradition, ideology and politics as usual.

Our second working principle has been to create new kinds of institutions that in their very design and activity challenge the foundations of their traditional "counterparts." Examples: The East Side Institute is an educational, research and training center for our new psychology of becoming. But anyone can study and train with us, no matter their educational level or profession. The Institute's educational approach is playful, philosophical and conversational, as opposed to didactic, and our goal is to support as diverse a group of people as possible to create developmental learning environments. The Barbara Taylor School, which I ran for 12 years, denied individuated, acquisitional learning, and where we began every school day with the question, "How shall we perform school today?" Our social therapy centers practice a group therapy approach that defies the medical model of mainstream psychotherapy and denies that emotionality is in our "heads," and, instead, locates emotionality in social activity. UX is a university-style adult school that is free, open to everyone who wants to participate and has no grades or degrees. The All Stars Talent Show is a national network of talent shows for youth that is based on cooperation, not competition and ignores the very conception of talent.

Today, the organizations that comprise what is now called the "development community" are the All Stars Project and its youth development programs, free developmental school for people of all ages, and its theatre; the East Side Institute for Group and Short Term Psychotherapy with its education and study programs and courses and research; the Social Therapy Group in NYC and social therapy affiliates in other cities; Performance of a Lifetime, a for-profit business that brings our performance approach to corporations and non-profits to "humanize" the workplace; independentvoting org; and the biennial Performing the World conferences.

Big Ideas and Revolutionary Activity

These organizations have national and international reach, with the direct participation of tens of thousands who impact on hundreds of thousands. They reach different people with different specific needs, but all share a methodology that involves people of all ages in the ongoing collective activity of creating new kinds of environments where they can be active performers of their lives.

I now turn to some illustrations of how all the insights about play and performance and learning and development I have just described have been put to use. My examples are from one of the organizations we've built—the All Stars Project. Through its performance-based youth development programs, the All Stars challenges the traditional psychological approaches to solving social problems, especially poverty, the lack of opportunity in poor communities and poor families, and violence.

The first project is Operation Conversation: Cops & Kids, a performance-based intervention on the intensely conflict-ridden relationship between police officers and young people of color in the US. Ten years ago, an especially brutal police shooting of an unarmed young man in NYC prompted Lenora Fulani, co-founder of the All Stars Project and a long-time political activist and grassroots educator, to try a new approach to the community's anger. She brought some police officers and inner-city teens to do something quite unusual—to improvise and perform together. Over the next 10 years well over 100 workshops have taken place in housing projects, community centers, churches, schools and Police Athletic League Centers, with about 2000 young people and 1500 police officers participating. Twice a year, there is a public demonstration of a workshop that all new police officers who have just graduated from the police academy must attend.

Operation Conversation: Cops and Kids

This is a scene from a workshop. The police officers and young people are creating a scene on a trivial topic—on this day it was pets—that has nothing to do with the tensions between them. Right before, they were walking around in slow motion, making funny faces at each other and talking in gibberish. After being silly and awkward with each other like this, the cops and kids sit down and talk. They tell each other what's hard about being a cop and what's hard about being a kid. They discover that what's hard is the same—worrying you won't come home alive. They also tell each other how they wish the cops would treat them and how they wish the kids would treat them. The cops and kids are creating new performances of themselves and of their relationship. They can see each other in new ways, not in their cop and kid social roles. It's play that allows them to experience each other as human beings, and to create more choices of how to act the next time they encounter each other in the streets.

Operation Conversation: Cops & Kids resists what American social psychologist Ken Gergen calls "the tyranny of the normal"—the normal ways of understanding and trying to alleviate tensions between law enforcement and young people. These include surveys, education on drug and violence prevention directed at youth, and sensitivity training directed at police. More broadly, it is an alternative to ways of understanding and resolving racism that derive from traditional psychology and sociology. The program disrupts normal ways of relating, which is as if we are fixed characters acting out an already scripted play. It disrupts a behaviorist psychology that insists what we can change is an individual's or a group's behavior. It disrupts cognitive approaches to dealing with tough social problems, which assume that if you learn the facts—how to have safe sex, what the traditions of a particular ethnic group are, or how to act when a policeman stops you—then the problem will vanish.

Framing and organizing the workshop as performatory, including directing the participants to perform both as themselves and as different characters, is the disruption. The workshop isn't designed to change anyone's behavior or to teach anything. Rather, it is designed to provide the young people and the police officers the opportunity to create together because in that process they might see, feel, think, speak and listen in ways they hadn't seen, felt, thought, spoken and/or listened before.

When they perform together, the young people and police officers have done something they have never done before. They have created a new piece of culture out of something in the broader culture and their separate subcultures. They have this new performance in their individual and collective experiences. They have added a new element to their overworked scripted ways of relating to each other. Having done that once, they could do it again. In the future they may or may not choose to exercise this performance option when they encounter each other on the street. But they now have that choice. Creating choices is how we grow. Performance is a means of growth because it gives people the license to make new choices of how to relate to oneself, to others and to the world.

Big Ideas and Revolutionary Activity

The young people and police officers are performing "a head taller" just like I mentioned earlier the way very young children do. They are playing with their identities by performing both who they are and who they are not—and experiencing that they did it. Creating the performance space and the performance—cops and kids performing moving slowly, performing improvisational skits, performing conversation and performing empathy—is a collective creative activity that is, for both the young people and the police officers. It is a venturing beyond "the narrow circle and narrow boundaries" of their own individual experience. Their experiences are broadened and with that, they have more choices for being/becoming.

Youth Onstage

The second All Stars program I want to tell you about is Youth Onstage, one of the programs of the All Stars. Youth Onstage introduces young people, ages 14 to 21, to performance, improvisation and the world of theatre. The training—all done by volunteer theatre professionals—is in the performing arts and emphasizes ensemble building. Graduates of Youth Onstage often appear in plays in conjunction with the All Stars' Castillo Theatre.

To give you a sense of the program and its impact, I tell a story of 7 young people from the program. They are poor and working class, African American and Latino, boys and girls. Two of them dropped out of high school and the rest go to some of the least successful schools in New York City.

On this particular evening, these 7 step onto a theatre stage. They perform a staged reading of the play *What is to be Dead?* by Fred Newman. The play, which was written for adult actors and audiences, engages issues of death, time, postmodernism, revolution, existentialism, and the relationship between blacks and Jews in the United States. The young people perform their reading of the play and then sit down for a conversation with the audience, mostly white adults. The adults ask a lot of questions— "What was it like for you, an African American boy, to play a Russian Jew in 19th century Russia?" "How did you learn your lines?" Do you know what the play was about?"

One of the young men, Ramik, responded like this: "I am not sure the play is about something, but it seems to me that Fred (Newman) was playing around with a lot of existential issues. Like, what is death? Is it an ending? And are we just one person, one true self?

Someone else asks him if he studied philosophy in school. All the young performers look at each other and laugh. When asked what's funny they describe schools where they barely read books, let alone have conversations on philosophy, and where their classes focus on trying to make up for what they hadn't been taught in elementary and middle school.

Ramik says, "I learned more in the three weeks of preparing for this reading than

I've learned all year in school, maybe ever. When we began reading the play, I could barely pronounce the words, but then I started to get really into the character and the lines started to make more sense. The director told us a lot about the history of Jews in Russia and communism and the history of Jews and Blacks working together. And then I started reading stuff online. And it's really interesting."

Ramik had not finished high school, his school reading level was not even close to the level of the theatrical play, and yet here he was conversing with adults about communism and death and his own learning process. He and the other young people were able to perform *What is to be Dead?* and to have such a conversation with the adult audience because they and the adults who worked with them in the program created a stage for them to perform a head taller, beyond their developmental level and way beyond their school learning. They were playing with language, doing what they didn't know how to do, performing who they were becoming.

For Ramik and the others, the performed activity of making theatre reinitiated their learning, their confidence as learners, and their desire to continue to learn. The how of play as performed activity is not just cognitive. It is equally emotional. This unity of cognition and emotion is critical in order for people, especially those young people who have essentially given up, to develop continuously as successful learners.

I have dozens and dozens more illustrations, and if we had time I would describe dozens more projects we and others who are following this approach are doing right now. Since we don't have all day, all I can do is give you a small glimpse some of the people who I've worked with over the decades building development activities and organizations, bringing play and performance back into people's lives. It has been a privilege to be part of an ongoing creative activity that is crossing the borders of nations, classes, cultures and ideologies and that is impacting on the development of tens of thousands of people all over the world.

I've learned and grown from the 8 year-old boy labeled autistic who became a co-therapist of a social therapy group. When the group ended he told the members, "I like that I can help people. I am no longer focusing on my problems. I like that. A way I could describe how the group has helped me is it has helped me live my life." From the 65 year-old retired health care worker who had given up her dream to be a writer decades earlier when she had to support and raise a disabled daughter. She literally wept when she realized she could take a playwriting workshop for free at the All Stars—and who went on to write a play about her teenage years in the slums of Manhattan's Lower East Side.

From the 17 year-old tough teenager from the South Bronx who, learning about improvisation in Youth Onstage! began to teach his friends to say "Yes/And" to whatever offers, however unwelcome, life dealt them in order to get beyond complaining to creating new possibilities. From the head of a major American oil fortune who gave $10 to one of our organizers on the street in the early 1990s and went

Big Ideas and Revolutionary Activity

on to become an influential advocate of our performance approach to development and to donate over $2 million to our organizing efforts. From the academics and practitioners in Sao Paulo, Brazil, Tokyo, Japan, Dhaka, Bangladesh, Pretoria, South Africa, Belgrade, Serbia, Juarez, Mexico and London, England who have been inspired to start organizing developmental activities in the poor communities in their cities. From the hundreds of educators, youth workers, medical and mental health people we have trained at the East Side Institute over the years. There's Peter Nsubuga from Uganda who started a village school outside Kampala knowing only that the children weren't developing, and how he, his program and his community have grown into practitioners of developmental performance. There's Ishita Sanyal and Prativa Sengupta, two Indian psychologists working in different ways with the mentally ill, who wanted at first to only restore to them some dignity and meaningful activity, but who came to experience the far greater potential of relating to these people in emotional distress as active creators and performers of their lives. There's Miguel Cortes and Jorge Burciaga in Cuidad Juárez, Mexico, among the most violent cities in the world, who opened the Fred Newman Center and organize and support people to transform the emotionality of fear into one of hope. And there's Elena Boukouvala, who brings young people in Greece's refugee camps together with native Greek youth to create music and art and meaningful relationships.

These and others have helped me to understand at a much deeper level than 40 years ago why play and performance are so powerful. It's because play isn't about what you do. It's about HOW you do what you do. We miss the importance of play in our lives if we think of it as what little children do with their toys and stuffed animals. What athletes do when they're on the football or baseball field. What actors do on the stage. What the rest of us do if we have leisure time, some friends, some musical instruments, a deck of cards, or a board game.

Play has to become a HOW. For all of us, but especially for people who've stopped growing—because of poverty, trauma, abuse, physical limitation and all the other reasons people stand still. People have to be able to play with the "hard stuff" of life, as my examples Operation Conversation: Cops & Kids and Youth Onstage played with hostility and with failing schools. I hope you could get a sense of how performing in new ways can reinitiate a love of learning, create new ways of relating to each other, generate hope, encourage, and empower. As a play revolutionary I invite people to play with anything and everything in their lives. That's because it generates choices: you can go to work, hang out with friends, do chores, study, have an argument, and so on, in the way you typically do (as who you "are") or you can engage in these life activities playfully, allowing yourselves to perform in new ways that help you discover that together, we can create more choices for how to be.

Engaging in any and all life activities playfully brings human development and community development together. It's how we get to belong to existing communities and also how we create new communities that meet our needs for learning and growing—that are development communities.

There's something very special about belonging to a community or a group that you were part of creating, that didn't exist before, that got built through you and others working and playing together. You not only have the community but you also have new kinds of relationships with your fellow builders, relationships nurtured and supported by the very community you built!

In the words of two young people who participated in performance programs:

> I've learned that community doesn't necessarily mean people who are like you. It's people who you do something with. (16 year-old girl)

> Before, community for me was just the people who live in your neighborhood. But I don't know anyone in my neighborhood really. We moved there three years ago and one of the few people I got to know moved. Now I think that community isn't who you live with, it's who you interact with. (17 year-old girl)

When people create developmental community they confront some paradoxes of contemporary life—and that's a good thing. The first paradox is this—life is lived socially, but is experienced and related to individualistically. The second paradox is this—life is continuous process, but is experienced and related to as products located in a particular time and space. The third paradox is this—people live, learn and develop in social units, but are not instructed in ways of creating or functioning effectively in them. People don't even know how to talk about such things. Conversations are rare among family members on HOW they want to live together, or among students and teachers on how they want to create their classroom, or among work groups on how they could function to maximize productivity and creativity, and so on.

We need to invite children, youth and adults to engage these paradoxes directly and practically. You have to have the experience of transforming what there is in order to create hope. How do we do that? By creating environments for people to participate in activities in which they will have to discover for themselves such things as how to create a group, what learning is, how to talk and listen and create a conversation.

My decades of experience have taught me that it is as performers that people are able to engage, in a developmental way, the paradox of experiencing what is a social existence as a separate and individuated one.

Children *become*, Vygotsky showed, through the performances as other than who they are (speakers, artists, readers, caregivers, and so on) that they and their caretakers create together. If children were not simultaneously being and becoming, there would be no human civilization. Little children do this without any awareness of it, they "create the ensemble" through their relational activity. Their performance as learners leads their development. But this human ability gets stifled as we become socialized to expe-

Big Ideas and Revolutionary Activity

rience ourselves as isolated individuals. It needs desperately to be rekindled. Conscious performance is a method to do so because it intensifies the relationship between being and becoming. Performance reminds us that we are social beings. Playing around with psychological jargon, I characterize the human developmental process as one of creating stages for development rather than going through stages of development.

I've touched on many themes, including: the gap in the world between our learning needs and our development needs; how play and performance can create developmental learning and development communities; and the need to engage life's paradoxes in order to reinitiate development and learning. I end by offering you what I think is one of the most significant statements about community I've ever heard. It's from a talk Fred Newman gave twenty-five years ago, and they guide me every day.

Newman told the audience that he was reading a popular and influential book called "The Family as a Haven in a Heartless World"—and that he didn't agree with it. So, he titled his talk "Community as a Heart in a Havenless World." Here's some of what he said:

> There is no haven, no place to hide. There is no escaping the cruelty, the pain, the torture. Many people try. They turn to families, to intellectual endeavor, to relationships, to drugs, to crime, people look to politics, people look everywhere to find a haven. People join communities because they seek a haven in a heartless world. But there is, in my opinion, no haven....I want to talk about community not as a location, but as an activity. Not as a haven, not as a place where we can go and hide. Community is the specific—and passionate—activity of supporting people who, far from seeking a haven in a heartless world, want to engage its cruelty, to do something to change it, to create a world in which havens are not necessary.
>
> *Fred Newman, 1990*

In other words, community of hope.

The Diagnostic Debate: Voices From the Street

Lois Holzman

With assistance from Brenda Perez Dominguez,
Matthew Gonzalez, Diana Guerra and Carrie Lobman
East Side Institute, New York NY eastsideinstitute.org

Part of a symposium, Beyond the DSM—Current Trends in Devising
New Diagnostic Alternatives, American Psychological Association
Annual Convention, August 8, 2015, Toronto Ontario

The Diagnostic Debate: Voices from the Street. For the past 40 years, Lois and her colleagues have spoken to thousands of people, both on the streets and through the internet, in an attempt to find out what people expect from therapy, the ways in which people play, what people want from their schools, what they believe their communities need, and more recently, how people feel about our current mental health system. By taking to the streets, getting people involved, and engaging in discourse about mental health with everyday people, they gathered a unique data set, which reveals that many people see the medical-model as outdated, isolating and in need of adjustment. The powerful responses shared within the surveys show a growing concern for the harmful effects of diagnosis and a longing for more community discourse and engagement when it comes to questions of emotional healing and growth.

I've been talking to strangers for 40 years. That's as long as I've had a PhD. I've spoken to many many thousands, maybe even a million, New Yorkers on the streets and at their doors. I've petitioned for candidates, invited people to participate in privately funded innovative youth programs and international conferences, and conducted surveys on many topics—what people expect from their therapists, how they play, what they think their communities need, what kind of schools they would like to see, and more. For the past four years, I and my colleagues and students have been on the streets talking to people about how they feel about the current mental health system.

I don't talk to strangers by myself. There's always a team. And we don't only talk to strangers but we invite and train others—students, clients, professional colleagues, volunteers and staff—to go out on the streets and create conversation with whoever will stop and talk with them. We give people lots of support to succeed—improv and ensemble-building exercises, role plays—and a good basic script.

This kind of community organizing is hard work and energizing at the same time.

Big Ideas and Revolutionary Activity

It's humbling—both being ignored and connecting with someone are two ways it puts you in touch with our humanity. It's incredibly informative—and challenging of assumptions about people you didn't even know you had. And it's a great antidote to cynicism—the overall experience is how grateful people are that someone wants to talk to them about these kinds of issues. I realize that I could have devoted this presentation entirely to this kind of community organizing—as a methodology of human and community development research and practice. Maybe next year. But for this symposium, let me turn to the issue at hand— diagnosis and alternatives to it.

My focus today is two-fold: our 2013 and 2014 street surveys, and the online version we launched two months ago. Survey on Emotional Distress and Mental Health Diagnoses http://goo.gl/forms/pMJdbRBxcf.

Who launched the surveys?
Two New York City based organizations that are proponents and practitioners of non-medical model understandings and practices:

- East Side Institute for Group and Short Term Psychotherapy
- Social Therapy Group

The Institute is a training, education and research center that develops a performatory, postmodern, group approach to human and community development and learning, and promotes other relational, cultural and critical approaches. The Institute has trained hundreds of psychologists, counselors, educators, social workers and performing arts activists from dozens of countries in social therapeutics.

The Social Therapy Group (socialtherapygroup.com) is a center for the practice of Social Therapy in Brooklyn and Manhattan with a client base of 175-200 people of all ages. There are affiliated centers in Atlanta, Boston, Philadelphia and other cities. Social Therapy is a non-diagnostic group approach that focuses on continued emotional development.

Reasons for the Surveys—A Brief History
—Our long-standing opposition to the medical model and diagnosis coupled with our 35-year practice of an effective non-diagnostic cultural-relational approach to therapy, training and supervision.

—Our commitment to community building as essential to emotional development and the involvement of people of all ages and walks of life in creating new ways of relating to "mental health," "mental illness," emotionality and the broader issues of human development and learning.

—An increased concern when in 2003 New York State legislated licensing requirements for therapists. Subsequent legislation was enacted restricting sites allowable for students and new practitioners to be supervised and get their hours. This resulted in a narrowing of treatment options—as well as understandings of emotional distress—available to the public

—The revision of the DSM generated significant controversy and was a hot topic among professionals and in the media. Informed and/or activist consumers, especially parents of children with a diagnosis of autism or Asperger's, took to the blogosphere. However, there's been little opportunity for the broader public to participate in this important dialogue. We know that in the past, efforts to change or eliminate the medicalization of specific "disorders" were successful because grassroots support was mobilized, as in the case of homosexuality.

—The biases of opinion polls. The few published public opinion studies I could find are forced choice and presume a medical model. Our surveys are open-ended. We want to learn from ordinary people—in their own words—how they are being impacted upon by the pervasiveness of the biologically-based diagnostic model—the bombardment by media and ad campaigns of the pharmaceutical companies, and the attempt to reduce stigma with a "mental problems are an illness" public service campaign—not to mention their visits to their physicians and local clinics, and meetings with the teachers, counselors and social workers at their neighborhood schools. What do they think they need? What would be effective ways to involve people in learning about alternatives and, for those who wanted more choices, in shaping new approaches in collaboration with us and other like-minded professionals?

The Street Surveys
The surveys were conducted at two annual NYC street fairs attended by millions of people: Harlem Week and Atlantic Antic. These fairs were chosen as locations with a strong and steady flow of traffic of people browsing and eager to see what the next booth would bring. In addition, we were seeking an ethnically diverse crowd with substantial African American and working class representation.

The surveys were conducted on Sunday afternoons. At each fair, the Institute and Social Therapy Group shared a booth that displayed literature, books and fliers. The booth was staffed by 5-6 people who fanned out and stopped walkers-by and asked them to talk. Conversations lasted from five to over ten minutes each. In all, 143 people participated in the survey in 2013 and 149 in 2014. They ranged in age from 15-80, with most being between 35-55. Roughly half were African Americans.

Results of the 2013 survey
The majority of people (60%) felt that diagnosis could be valuable, especially in providing relief to know "what's wrong."

Ninety percent of those who said diagnosis could be helpful had serious reservations—only sometimes, danger of misdiagnosis, the racism of diagnosis, stigma, leads to over-medication. These were the same kinds of things the 40% who said diagnosis wasn't helpful said. There was a particular vehemence against drugs for children.

Big Ideas and Revolutionary Activity

> "Medication makes you act out. My grandson was hyperactive, not ADHD, and they wanted to put him on Ritalin – I told them no."

> "Kids get told in 1st grade they're crazy—then it becomes a self-fulfilling prophecy."

The 2014 Survey

In 2014, we tried to go a little deeper and see if we could help people explore the apparent conflict around diagnosis, i.e., its value and its dangers. We also wanted to learn what they thought about the necessity and mandate of diagnosis.

Sixty percent of respondents said people did not need a diagnosis to get help with their emotional pain. Of those who said diagnosis was needed, nearly all said it was the only way to get to talk to someone. They overwhelmingly said we shouldn't consider such people as having a brain disorder or chemical imbalance.

Across the board (whether they said diagnosis was needed or not), people again expressed concerns about diagnosis—the stigma, the dangers of misdiagnosis, and over-medication.

> "Once you have that label it doesn't stay at the clinic. You carry it with you for a long time."

> "People start calling you crazy. It can be a shame for the family."

> "Getting a diagnosis limits life experience, you're treated differently, you feel like an outcast."

> "It's good to know what's wrong, but it might make them feel worse about themselves and put them in a box."

Three months later in December 2014, we held a public event, "Do Diagnostic Labels Determine Who We Are?" Forty people attended the event, including some we had met doing the surveys. The conversation lasted two hours and the mostly working-class adults who participated shared experiences and opinions about drug companies, the school system and mental health clinics; how they felt about having this kind of conversation; and responses to hearing from the facilitator about alternative ways to understand and deal with emotional pain and ways to relate to diagnosis.

We had a written exit poll at the end of the forum. All forty participants answered yes to "This conversation on diagnosis and labeling made me think about some things in new ways." Here's a small sample of what people wrote in response to "What's something you might share with a friend?"

> "I will be sharing everything with a friend especially the importance of labeling and how powerful that can be or damaging."

> "To encourage people to speak more publicly about the topic of mental illness and alternatives to medication and treatment."

"The political consequences of diagnosis."

"The importance of being social and developing as a social being with a community of people."

"Stop worrying about the diagnosis and focus on what you can create with it."

Participants were enthusiastic and asked for more events like this one. Thirteen of the 40 participants asked to volunteer as future survey takers.

The success of our pilot street surveys and the positive response to a written report on it from colleagues within the DxSummit and beyond spurred us on to tweak the survey and make it available to anyone who wanted to use it and take it—by posting it online and inviting others to post it, print it out, spread the word across the globe.

The Survey on Emotional Distress and Mental Health Diagnosis— Early Results and What We're Learning

The survey was put online in late May of this year. It consists of seven open-ended questions and requests for demographic information.

As of now, it has been sent to the 10,000 people in the Institute's and Social Therapy Group's data base, the Future of Mental Health data base, posted on Dx Summit, Mad in America, my blog at Psychology Today, dozens of Facebook, Twitter, LinkedIn accounts, and postings by individuals. It's been translated into Portuguese and Spanish by colleagues in Brazil and NYC.

What We've Got

As of August 2, 2015, 404 people completed surveys online.

They are overwhelmingly from the US but we have surveys from 21 other countries. They range in age from teens through the 80s, with 60% in their 30s to 60s. They are mostly urban and female. 68% are white. We were surprised at how many of them asked to be contacted for a follow-up conversation—62%.

At this point, we've done some basic coding of a little more than half the surveys. From these preliminary results, responses look similar to the street surveys. More than half said diagnosis isn't needed. More than half said diagnosis was both harmful and helpful and 25% said it was harmful. This comment sums it up:

> "I think it depends on the individual. Certainly, getting a diagnosis can help a person get their insurance to pay for therapy, so that is helpful. I think some people need explanations, find it a relief, so I guess that would be helpful. One problem is that people can so easily become their diagnosis—that is harmful, and can even be stigmatized."

Both online and on the street, we also asked people about alternatives to diagnosis.

Big Ideas and Revolutionary Activity

To the question, "What do you think are ways to help people in emotional pain?" people had a lot to say—from talking to people (friends, family and therapists) to social or community building activities like volunteering, dance, art, to exercise, meditation and yoga. One person said this:

> "What we need is more facilities where people can walk in and say 'Hey, I'm feeling really down today. Can I just be here for a while and see what could be a contribution to me and make me feel better?' I think this is true for most people but especially young people."

In response to the question, "Are you aware of approaches or professionals that don't use diagnosis?" seventy five percent said no (which means we have our work cut out for us).

Our last question could be the most relevant to you here today. We asked, "Do you have any other thoughts you would like to share with mental health professionals around the world who are exploring alternatives to diagnosis and developing ways to help people emotionally? What would you like to say to them?"

Here's what people, both on the streets and online, had to say:

There were dozens of versions of the following—
>   Treat people with respect
>
>   Stop with the pharmaceutical "fixes"
>
>   Everyone is different
>
>   Context matters
>
>   Keep it up!

And a few choice quotes:
> "Don't be constrained by what is. So many breakthroughs in human history are the result of folks cutting against the grain of what is. Dare to question established wisdom and convention."
>
> "Don't come up with another way to label."
>
> "Find a way to create a culture where talking about emotional upheaval and emotional problems is accepted and open outside of diagnosis."
>
> "Play with diagnosis if you must have diagnosis. But don't believe that it is 'truth.'"
>
> "We should be making the range of 'normal' bigger—not smaller."

And perhaps the most telling comment:
> "Keep including us."

Next weekend my teams and I will be on the streets talking to strangers. How moralizing it would be if I can report from APA that psychologists from across the US and Canada are including them. I hope you make that possible.

Appendix: Online Survey and Responses
(based on first 229 surveys submitted)

Survey on emotional distress and mental health diagnoses

We are conducting research on how people think about emotional distress and mental health diagnoses. We are a group of researchers and practitioners who are concerned about our mental health system. We believe that a variety of mental health approaches should be available to people from all walks of life.

During the last few years more and more mental health professionals around the world are talking to each other about diagnosing people who are experiencing emotional distress. They're concerned about the impact of giving and receiving a diagnosis, and the diagnostic system that is used in clinics, hospitals and private practices.

These discussions are primarily among professionals. We think this very important conversation needs the community's voice.

We want to hear from you! We will make use of your responses to create a more vibrant and open dialogue.

Please take a moment to take our survey. Your responses are completely anonymous.

* Required

Big Ideas and Revolutionary Activity

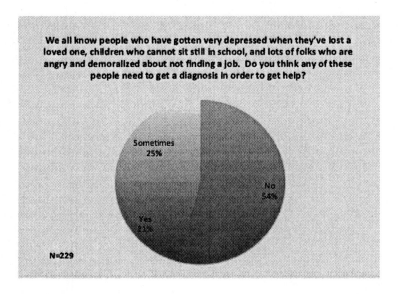

Some quotes:

"NO! That is ridiculous. Diagnosis was invented by and for the insurance and pharmaceutical companies not for the people who are in emotional pain."

"I think I do—in order to provide treatment, it makes sense that it relate to a diagnosis. I would hope that the diagnosis could include "signs of depression" or "feelings of anxiety— this doesn't require a clinical label, but acknowledges an unhealthy mental state that can be further addressed through counseling."

"No, I don't agree at all. There is over diagnosing in this country to pad the pockets of the healthcare system. For example, a lot of African-American children are diagnosed with ADHD and then placed in self-contained classrooms where they fail even more, when in fact there could have been many different ways to intervene on why the child could not stay still in class."

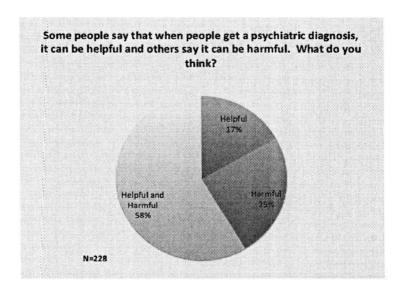

Some quotes:

"I think it depends on the individual. Certainly, getting a diagnosis can help a person get their insurance to pay for therapy, so that is helpful. I think some people need explanations, find it a relief, so I guess that would be helpful. One problem is that people can so easily become their diagnosis--that is harmful, and can even be stigmatized."

"It might be helpful, but it might also be harmful. Really depends on the full context. The client/consumer should get a say in it. Unfortunately, the way our society is currently structured, getting away from this kind of labeling is almost impossible."

Big Ideas and Revolutionary Activity

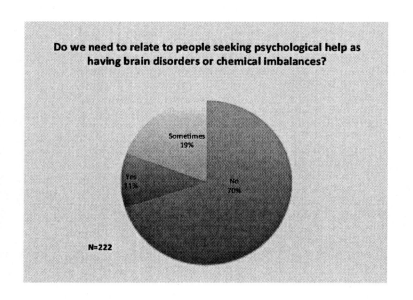

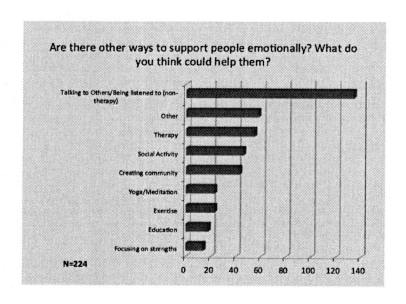

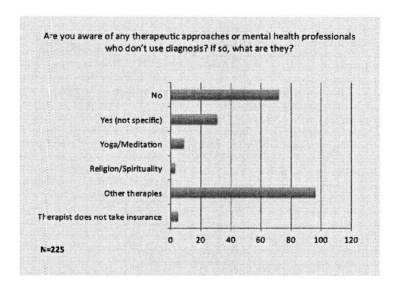

Big Ideas and Revolutionary Activity

Social Therapy and Creating an Activist Life

In **Social Therapy and Creating an Activist Life** Lois shares the decades she has spent organizing environments that promote the transformation of relationships. Through social therapeutics, Lois and her colleagues work with groups large and small to reactivate hope and imagination by reminding us of our human capacity to self-organize in order to meet our needs. She invites us to become active creators of our relationality, our emotionality and our growth by exercising our power to create something new together. In this way, social therapeutics is ever-evolving, fluid and emergent, exploring the dialectical unities of individual-society and cognition-emotion. For Lois and her colleagues, development is a sociocultural activity, something that we create rather than something that happens to us. This position releases development from its institutionalized bindings, shifting the focus from the authority of knowing to the power of creativity.

We have been taught to believe that the past determines the present. Karl Marx challenged this—and posited that it doesn't have to be that way, that the present can determine the past. This has been one of the inspirations of my life.

Another inspiration is found in the words of Dr. Martin Luther King, Jr.—words about psychology and about social injustice.

> You who are in the field of psychology have given us a great word. It is the word maladjusted. It is certainly good to declare that destructive maladjustments should be destroyed. But I am sure that we will recognize that there are some things in our society, some things in our world, to which we should never be adjusted. There are some things concerning which we must always be maladjusted if we are to be people of good will. We must never adjust ourselves to racial discrimination and racial segregation. We must never adjust ourselves to religious bigotry. We must never adjust ourselves to economic conditions that take necessities from the many to give luxuries to the few. We must never adjust ourselves to the madness of militarism and the self-defeating effects of physical violence.
>
> Thus, it may well be that our world is in dire need of a new organization, The International Association for the Advancement of Creative Maladjustment. Men and women should be as maladjusted as the prophet Amos, who in the midst of the injustices of his day, could cry out in words that echo across the centuries, "Let justice roll down like waters and righteousness like a mighty stream"; or as maladjusted as Abraham Lincoln, who in the midst of his vacillations finally came to see that this nation could not survive half slave

Big Ideas and Revolutionary Activity

and half free; or as maladjusted as Thomas Jefferson, who in the midst of an age amazingly adjusted to slavery, could scratch across the pages of history, words lifted to cosmic proportions, "We hold these truths to be self-evident, that all men are created equal. That they are endowed by their creator with certain inalienable rights. And that among these are life, liberty, and the pursuit of happiness." And through such creative maladjustment, we may be able to emerge from the bleak and desolate midnight of man's inhumanity to man, into the bright and glittering daybreak of freedom and justice. (from a speech delivered to the American Psychological Association in 1967)

I've been asked to share with you what I do and how I came to be doing it. To tell you about the independent path I—an academically trained research psychologist—and my colleagues have taken to create opportunities for growth and development for people and their communities. To organize environments that involve all kinds of people—young and old, rich, poor and in-between—in transforming their relationships to themselves, to each other and to the institutional gatekeepers of both local and global culture. To re-initiate hope and imagination through exercising our human capacity to self-organize to meet our needs. To support people to become active creators of their relationality, their emotionality, their learning. To remake the world in such a way that everyone can have what they need to continue to develop themselves and their communities.

The work we do doesn't fit into any known categories and so it goes by many names—social therapeutics, the psychology of becoming, the development community, performance activism, postmodern Marxism are some of the most recent. Social therapeutics because it is grounded in Fred Newman's creation of social therapy 40 years ago. A psychology of becoming because it takes human beings to be not just who we are but simultaneously who we are becoming. The development community because it engages in the activity of creating development and the activity of creating the community that supports development. Performance activism because its politics is one of reconstruction and transformation through people creating new performances of themselves. Postmodern Marxism because it is inspired by Marx's revolutionary philosophy and radical humanism of transforming the very circumstances that determine us through the all-round development of everyone—and by the postmodern questioning of the tenets of modernism including truth, reality and objectivity. As postmodern Marxists, we don't interpret, predict, commodify, define or deconstruct. Instead, we create new, ever-evolving organizations and programs—in and through which people can exercise their power to create something new, to become historical even as they remain societal, to embrace the individual-group dialectic rather than assume a separate individual and group in opposition to each other, to transform how we do everything.

This revolutionary activity of ours is realized, manifested and developed through a network of independent organizations that we have built and expanded over 40 years.

Two guiding principles were there at the start and remain to this day. First, to be independently funded and supported, and not take money from or be constrained by government, corporate, university, foundation or other traditional funding sources. This involved reaching out to ordinary Americans for financial support and participation, by stopping them on street corners and knocking on the doors of their homes. That activity allowed individuals to become active participants in the activities and organizations we were building together. And because we reached out to all sorts of people on the streets and by knocking on their doors, what has evolved is a new kind of partnership between wealthy Americans and the poor, a partnership that sidesteps the institutions and assumptions of tradition, ideology and politics as usual.

Our second working principle has been to create new kinds of institutions that in their very design and activity challenge the foundations of their traditional "counterparts." Some examples: a labor union for welfare recipients (unemployed people) who did not labor and, therefore, were at no point of production; a school for children that denied the individuated, knowledge-seeking model of learning that is the bedrock of schooling East and West; therapy centers with an approach to emotional help that denies that emotionality is in our "heads," that, instead, locates emotionality in social activity and that defies the medical model of mainstream psychotherapy; a "university" that is free, open to everyone who wants to participate and has no grades or degrees; a national network of talent shows for youth that is based on cooperation, not competition, and denies the very conception of talent; electoral political campaigns that are not concerned with winning and political parties that exist to transform political culture—including the possibility of doing away with political parties altogether and creating more direct and democratic modes of citizen participation.

Today, the organizations that comprise what is now called the "development community" are the All Stars Project and its youth development programs—the All Stars Talent Show Network, Youth Onstage!, the Development School for Youth, and Operation Conversation: Cops and Kids; a university-style development school (UX) and political theatre (Castillo Theatre); the East Side Institute for Group and Short Term Psychotherapy; the Social Therapy Group in NYC and social therapy affiliates in other cities; Performance of a Lifetime, a for-profit business that brings our performance approach to corporations and non-profits to "humanize" the workplace; independentvoting org; and the biennial Performing the World conferences. These organizations have national and international reach, with the direct participation of tens of thousands who impact on hundreds of thousands. They reach different people with different specific needs, but all share a methodology that involves people of all ages in the ongoing collective activity of creating new kinds of environments where they can be active performers of their lives. This methodology "practically-critically" engages the institutions of psychology, education, and politics and their impact on people's daily lives.

Specifically, it brings the issue of human development into the institutions of mental

Big Ideas and Revolutionary Activity

health, social services, education, health-care community development, and politics where the topic and concern are shockingly absent. Not the mainstream understanding of human development, as going from inside out in a series of pre-determined stages. To us, development is a social-cultural-activity, something human beings create rather than something that happens to them. This cuts development loose from the meta-narratives of teleology and ideology, from the notion of progression from one stage to another, and from the idea of progress to some greater good. And without a meta-narrative explaining and constraining human activity, the focus can move from the authority of knowing to the power of creativity, from the glorification of the mythic isolated individual to the embracing of the relationality of life, from the need for instrumental and adaptive behavior to the need for the revolutionary becoming-ness of performance. Development becomes a practice of method, the process of organizing ways for people to create new ways to relate to each other, to the environments we are in, to culture, to community and to social change.

Performance plays a central role in this new psychology. By performance I mean the capacity we all have to pretend, to play. Like actors on the theatrical stage, we all can perform other than who we are. Not only can we, **we must** or else we would not ever learn anything or grow up. For performing as other than who they are is what babies do. They perform as speakers before they know how to speak. We encourage them. We pretend they are making sense. We pretend they understand what we are saying. And by playing this way, performing this way, pretending this way, they become speakers.

All of the work we do in the US and around the world is based in this simple but profound discovery: we develop and learn when we are allowed to perform, when others relate to us—and we learn to relate to ourselves and others—as simultaneously who we are and other than who we are.

As an academically trained linguist and developmental psychologist, how did I come to be a leader of this work? It's simple, really—I was asked, invited, organized. Just as I wasn't primed from an early age to be a scholar—no one in my family had been to university and I didn't even know there were such things as intellectuals—I didn't know there were people who devoted their lives to changing the world. Once I met political activists and community organizers, that's when I discovered it was what I wanted to become.

Over many years, I have been able to be a part of creating something qualitatively new, by leaving the institutional and conceptual constraints of the academy and bringing the best of its ideas and discoveries with me to be transformed into practical tools for ordinary people. Fred Newman, the architect of our work and my intellectual mentor and partner and close friend until he passed away in 2011, left the university in 1968. I left in 1997, keeping my academic location for the first two decades of our working together. We did our intellectual work in a unique and wonderfully creative multi-disciplinary environment that was inseparable from community organizing. We wrote books and articles and presented at professional and academic conferences, inviting scrutiny of our practices and dialogue about our discoveries. All the while, we were attracting more and more grassroots and independent activists and activist scholars like ourselves, including many from countries outside the US. In order to have an impact, it's vital, I believe, to bring cutting edge practices and methodologies from the grassroots to scholars and vice versa.

One way to characterize the life-long journey I've been on is as an ongoing transformation of the relationship between researcher and organizer. Researcher and organizer have some things in common. Both are essentially creative activities. Both involve bringing a grouping of people together for a common purpose. Researchers create in order to have something to say about the process, the results and/or the participants. As a young psychologist, I was a researcher who organized people in order to discover some things that might contribute to the knowledge base and ultimately be helpful to people, and to share that with others. Organizers, on the other hand, create things that you and the people you're organizing have ownership of, and value. As an organizer your task is to directly activate people to create something, to change what is into something that's becoming. Any discoveries that are made are inseparable from the organizing activity, inseparable from the activity of creating whatever the people are creating. My journey has been from being a researcher who organizes to becoming an organizer who researches. Instead of organizing people enough to do good research, I now research enough to do good organizing.

I will try to bring this journey to life for you by telling you about four mentors who had a profound influence on me.

My first mentor was Lois Bloom, a researcher and teacher who I worked with in the mid 1970s when I was a graduate student in the developmental psychology program at Columbia University. Lois taught me that to learn how children learn to speak and develop language we had to leave the laboratory and go into their homes and play groups. We had to spend time with toddlers, playing with them, talking with them, performing with them. I learned that context matters, that children don't do the same things in a laboratory that they do at home, that their talk is coordinated with what they are doing and who and what they are doing it with. I learned from working with Lois that qualitative research can be as rigorous—indeed, more rigorous—than quantitative research. Lois helped me to love research. She projected me out of the lab, and that has been the foundation of everything I have done since.

My second mentor, with whom I did post-doctoral work at Rockefeller University in the late 1970s, was Michael Cole. Mike taught me that laboratory experiments on human cognition cannot be ecologically valid because you can't see the social-cultural nature of cognition in the lab. He was also the first person to make me aware that science in general, and the social sciences and psychology in particular, are political and that the research we psychologists do can be practically relevant. And Mike introduced me to that very practical and very political social scientist, Lev Vygotsky. Both of those introductions—to Vygotsky and to the political nature of psychology—set the stage for my third

Big Ideas and Revolutionary Activity

mentor, Fred Newman, whom I've already mentioned.

I met Fred when I was completing my dissertation and beginning to work with Cole. Fred was a philosopher who had left academia during the late 1960s to do political and community organizing. He also had created a radical type of therapy, social therapy, informed by his background in philosophy of science and Marxism. Fred taught me many things through the decades of our continuous collaboration. One thing he did was give me a way into the world. Lois Bloom and Mike Cole both encouraged me to leave the laboratory. But while we may have been sitting in a playroom or family living room instead of a university lab, we brought the experimental mindset and method of the laboratory with us. What Fred showed me was a way to take the lab out of life. He invited me to develop a way to study the world through actively engaging in changing it. With Fred, I came to realize that my passion for human development came not just from intellectual curiosity but also from my belief that human beings must find a way to develop if our species is to survive and thrive, and from my desire to contribute to this revolutionary activity.

Working with Fred for 35 years not only transformed what I do; it also transformed who I am. I feel I am a better scientist for being a builder and co-creator of what I study, a better researcher for getting the laboratory out of life. What I learned with Bloom and Cole—the socio-cultural situatedness of learning and development, the need for psychology to be ecologically valid, the political nature of psychology, the contemporary significance of Lev Vygotsky—has been deepened and developed by virtue of being taken out of academia and brought into the lives of ordinary people.

My fourth mentor wasn't an individual. It was, and remains, the thousands of people who I've worked with over the decades building independent development activities and organizations. It's the 8-year-old boy labeled autistic who became a co-therapist of a social therapy group. When the group ended he told the members, "I like that I can help people. I am no longer focusing on my problems. I like that. A way I could describe how the group has helped me is it has helped me live my life." It's the 65-year-old retired health care worker who had given up her dream to be a writer decades earlier when she had to support and raise a disabled daughter. She literally wept when she realized she could take a playwriting workshop for free at the All Stars UX—and who went on to write a play about her teenage years in the slums of Manhattan's Lower East Side. It's the 17-year-old tough teenager from the South Bronx who learning about improvisation in Youth Onstage! began to teach his friends to say "Yes, and..." to whatever offers, however unwelcome, life dealt them in order to get beyond complaining to creating new possibilities. It's the New York City police officers who through our Operation Conversation: Cops and Kids program play theatre games and improvise silly skits with poor young people of color as a means of creating an atmosphere where the cops and kids can actually have a meaningful and growthful conversation. It's the head of a major American oil fortune who gave $10 to one of our organizers on the street in the early 1990s and went on to become an influential advocate of our performance approach to development and to donate over $2 million to our organizing efforts. It's the academics and practitioners in Sao Paulo, Brazil, Tokyo, Japan, Dhaka, Bangladesh, Pretoria, South Africa, Belgrade, Serbia and London, England who have been inspired to start organizing developmental activities in the poor communities of their cities. It's the hundreds of educators, youth workers, medical and mental health people we have trained over the years. Like Peter Nsubuga from Uganda who started a village school outside Kampala knowing only that the children weren't developing, and how he, his program and his community have grown into practitioners of developmental performance. Like Ishita Sanyal and Prativa Sengupta, two Indian psychologists working in different ways with the mentally ill, who wanted at first to only restore to them some dignity and meaningful activity, but who came to experience the far greater potential of relating to these people in emotional distress as active creators and performers of their lives. Like Miguel Cortes and Jorge Burciaga in Cuidad Juárez, Mexico, one of the most violent cities in the world, who opened the Fred Newman Center to organize and support people to transform the emotionality of fear into one of hope.

These individuals and countless others have taught me so much about the development that comes from diverse people self-organizing new activities and building new organizations in response to what they want and need. What I have learned from my fourth mentor could not have been learned had I remained exclusively within the university system, because what we have built could not have been created there. My first two mentors came from the academy. My third, Newman, came from the university and showed me, through example, the importance of taking the most advanced ideas and discoveries of the university to diverse communities of ordinary people. By becoming an organizer who researches what I'm helping to organize—independent of established institutions and funding sources—I have been able to be part of, and provide leadership to, an ongoing creative activity that is crossing the borders of nations, classes, cultures and ideologies, and that is impacting on the development of tens of thousands of people all over the world.

Let me end by emphasizing that this is not a journey I, or you, can do on your own. It's only possible through the shared commitment of a group of people who support each other to risk doing what they don't know how to do. Because if we are serious about creating new, developmental activities we need to realize that we can't know, in advance, what they will turn out to be. The independent path is not a knowable path. Nor is it an easy path. There are those at the university, in politics, in mainstream culture who will scorn your efforts and even attempt to derail your work. There will be times when you're not sure how to continue, but if you build a group that is dedicated to building groups, if your group keeps developing what (and who) develops, the impact can be profound on your life and the lives of so many others. From where I stand, the world looks stuck. To get unstuck we need to take some developmental risks.

Big Ideas and Revolutionary Activity

Vygotsky on the Margins: A Global Search for Method

Presented at the Symposium, Vygotsky and Social Justice: Community Education and Community Development, AERA Annual Meeting, Chicago, April 2015.

In **Vygotsky on the Margins: A Global Search for Method** Lois asserts that the Vygotsky she knows is quite different from the one brought forth in more traditional conceptions of development and education. At the margins, Vygotskians working outside the constraints of institutionalized academics are creating a revolution from the bottom up, taking the form of community organizers, youth workers, therapists and educators to name a few. Through the constant outreach, support and involvement of Lois and her colleagues, a global collective of activity-ists in almost 40 countries around the world are working together to form a community education project that is interdisciplinary, non-institutional and unique in its ever-evolving, ever-expanding community of development. Utilizing Vygotsky's tool-and-result methodology, a dialectical approach that centers on the unity/totality/whole in which method is actively practiced, not passively applied, they have learned that empowerment can be found when we (re)establish our ability to transform the determining circumstances in our lives. Such methodology promotes the collective healing to be found when we begin to look at development as a sociocultural activity rather than an individual accomplishment.

The Vygotsky that's been spreading around the world outside the university is primarily a developmentalist and not an educational psychologist. The key features of this Vygotsky were first articulated by Fred Newman and myself in our 1993 book *Lev Vygotsky: Revolutionary Scientist* and my 2009 *Vygotsky at Work and Play*. While these and other writings of ours are known by scholars, the main impact of our work has been on community organizers, youth workers, educators and counselors working outside the academy—many of them at the grass roots with poor and otherwise marginalized groups —children in the favelas of Brazil, men in South African prisons, mentally ill people in India, and families in violence-ridden Juarez Mexico, to name a few.

These people have come to know Vygotsky and been supported to make use of his method and discoveries through the constant outreach of my colleagues and I at the East Side Institute, a non-profit research, education and training center located in NYC that reaches out to the US and around the globe to bring the most innovative and cutting-edge approaches from academia to the field and vice versa. If there is to be a way out of the human development crisis we all face, it's ordinary people who are going to make it happen.

Big Ideas and Revolutionary Activity

The Institute has over twenty years experience in collaborating with hundreds of NGOs and individual scholars and community educators and activists in nearly 40 countries through its study and training programs, international conferences and institutional partnerships.

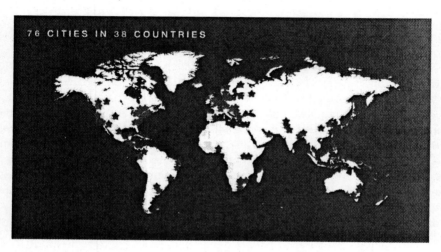

Approximately 75 relationships have been sustained for five years or more and are ongoing. A subset of the 75 are connected to each other and to the Institute as a means of support and ongoing development of their work. Together, they form a community education project that is unusual in being global, cross-disciplinary and non-university based. Perhaps its most unique feature is that it is an ever-expanding development community. By that I mean a community that supports the development of people and communities through its own continuous development. It is designed for people to self-organize in whatever ways make sense to them in their environments, to create new forms of life by activistically transforming the existing forms of life that stifle their development and learning.

Before I introduce some of these activists for development to you, let me summarize the key features of the Vygotsky they are inspired by and make use of. First is Vygotsky's method. As he was trying to create a new psychology in the early years of the Soviet Union, Vygotsky broke with the accepted scientific paradigm in which method is something to be applied in order to yield results—in other words, a tool for result. He put forth a different conception of method—not a tool to be applied, but an activity that generates both tool and result at the same time and as continuous process. In this case, tool and result are elements of a dialectical unity/totality/whole in which method is to be practiced, not applied—what Newman and I call tool-and-result methodology. Here is how he put it: "The search for method becomes one of the most important problems of the entire enterprise of understanding the uniquely human forms of psychological activity. In this case, the method is simultaneously prerequisite and product, the tool and the result of the study" (Vygotsky, 1978, p. 65).

Tool-and-result is also a way to understand human life. Individual, cultural and species development is created by human activity, which is qualitative and transformative (unlike behavior change, which is particularistic and cumulative). People do not merely respond to stimuli, acquire societally determined and useful skills, and adapt to the determining environment. The uniqueness of human social life is that we ourselves transform the determining circumstances. Human development is not an individual accomplishment but a *socio-cultural activity*. In my work, "tool-and-result" has helped me to see that people experience the social nature of their existence and the power of collective creative activity in the process of making new tools for growth (Holzman, 2009). Studying this activity and experience is likewise a transformation of existing circumstances.

Among the discoveries of Vygotsky's search for method that this global group of activists for development put into practice are: 1) his understanding of learning, or education, and development as a dialectical unity rather than as in linear or causal relation; 2) his concept of the zone of proximal development, or ZPD, as something that is created through people's activity rather than as a spatio-temporal entity; and 3) his understanding of what makes play developmental.

These key features form the methodology of social therapeutics, the name given to the Institute's approach. As a cultural approach to human life, it relates to human beings as the creators of our culture and ensemble performers of our lives; and to human and community learning and development as the social-cultural activity of creating "development zones/stages" where people can "become" through performing, as Vygotsky says, "a head taller" (Vygotsky, 1978, p. 102).

I'd like to introduce you to a few of our partners in this development project.

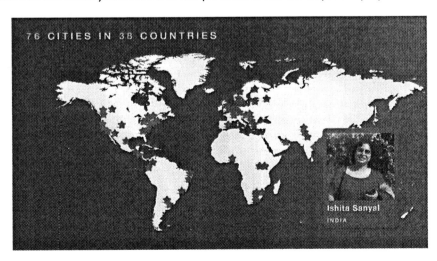

Big Ideas and Revolutionary Activity

Ishita Sanyal is one of the few psychologists in India. She lives in Kolkata. When her brother had a schizophrenic break she was faced with the stark reality that there were precious few services for people with severe mental illness, and none that gave them any dignity. So, she founded her own organization, Turning Point. At the beginning Ishita focused on involving people in educational activities, like computer training. This in itself was a big step, as what was available in other places was so-called occupational therapy such as bookbinding and pickle making. But being introduced to Vygotsky's method through the Institute, and meeting hundreds of people who were utilizing creative and performance activities in their work around the world, Ishita began to involve her staff and clients in developmental activities. She recognized that in order to reinitiate development and growth in people suffering from mental illness, you had to relate to them, in Vygotsky's sense, as a head taller through play. Over the years, since 2007, she has introduced readings on human development to them, helped them create skits from these readings and their life experiences, and taught them improv games. They even put on a show in the village square. The experience of being related to doing what they don't know how to do and what no one expects of them, of working collectively to create their growth, of succeeding, being appreciated and being seen as a human being has been transformative.

Recently, Ishita wrote to us about a talent show Turning Point organized for people with mental illness. She said: "At the initial screening we saw people complaining of headaches and becoming restless. But when the performance started they became increasingly enthusiastic and often performed more than once, not for the sake of competition, but for the pleasure of performing and discovery. They were able to create a completely different and more positive environment together where instead of only thinking about their problems and difficulties they were immersed in creatively praising each other. I think this helped them to grow and develop because they went from *I can't* to *I can*."

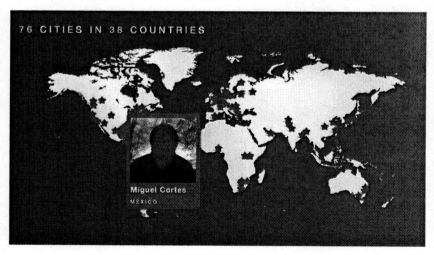

Miguel Cortes from Cuidad Juarez in Mexico is a community educator and non-diagnostic therapist.

"Four years ago, I was struggling to adjust myself to working at the University. I dreamt of doing community work but had no idea of how to do it, my friend was trying to find people he could work creatively with, and now, through totally different paths we come to be involved in doing community work with youth. And so, we now cannot only play drums together, we can now record albums created by youth, we can create workshops about comics that reflect life in Juarez, and so many other things. In just 4 years we have created conditions where we can do things unimaginable before. And it wasn't by reading the *"Seven steps for successful community building"* or *"Community building for dummies."* It was our growing and playing and creating community, it was participating in creating with our groups which is not a "let's all hold hands" kind of thing, but a huge struggle, of us at times having no idea what we were doing, of people leaving our community, of finding ways of continuing our work even when the conditions don't exist for it. You cannot appreciate Vygotsky deeply if you are not building with him, if you are not creating environments for growth."

Peter Nsubuga is a community worker in Kampala, Uganda. While in the UK studying accounting, Peter saw a TV show on the plight of children in Africa. He returned home to respond to the need for help in communities suffering from disease, extreme poverty, and lack of clean water. He himself grew up poor and had lost three brothers and one sister to AIDS. In 2008, Peter founded Hope for Youth, an organization that provides food, clothing, education and social-emotional development experiences to children and families in a remote area of Kampungu village in the Mukono District. Hope for Youth started with seven children under a tree, and today cares for over 250 children between 4-14 years in their school program, and over 50 youth and women in play and performance-based out-of-school programs.

Big Ideas and Revolutionary Activity

Commenting on what he learned and now practices, Peter says, "It's an eye opener to me on how we can continuously create development in our communities by becoming creators of changes instead of just passively watching life passing by. This is unique especially to those of us who were used to the system that was only encouraging us to be who we are, to develop our identities, rather than to continue performing as who we were becoming."

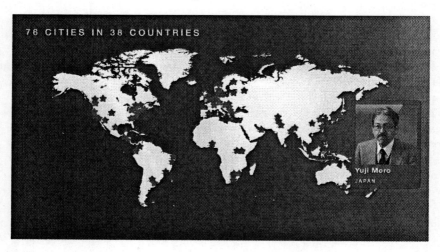

Yuji Moro is a prominent developmental psychologist in Japan who had been following cultural historical research since the early 1980s when his colleagues visited Mike Cole's lab in San Diego. Coming in contact with the Institute and Vygotsky as a developmentalist, he has come to recognize that human development can only come about through community development, and he's become a community activist. Among the projects he has implemented in the past five years are radical changes in university education that brings creativity and performance into the classrooms and collaborations with community organizations in Tokyo's poorest neighborhoods to re-initiate development in the most marginalized of teens and young adults.

Yuji recently commented on the impact of the revolutionary Vygotsky in Japan: "In the past few years, he's been an omnipresent figure, provoking academics into discussion on the unity of learning and development in conference rooms, on working as a community builder in various cities and countries, and on making stages for young people beginning their future."

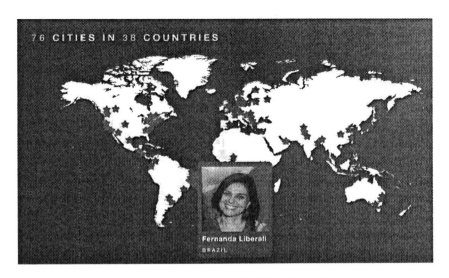

Fernanda Liberali uses her location at the applied linguistics department at a university in Sao Paulo Brazil to build community. She and her colleagues have built what they call the Creative Chain, an action research network across Brazil of teacher educators, students, teachers and administrators who practice a Vygotskian pedagogy. Over the past ten years, they've been transitioning from being primarily educators to community organizers focused on supporting children and families in the favelas to create and participate in self-organizing developmental experiences that bring them into the wider world of what their country has to offer.

As Fernanda puts it, "We have lived as a very poor country for a very long time, and now we are experiencing a new situation in the country. Since Lulu's election in 2002 we felt that things are different, and we could move beyond. People thought that they could develop, they could change, they could go ahead. After a while people thought that this was enough. But the enough was not enough. Because what people thought was enough was what they knew. But as Spinoza says, 'You can only want what you know.' But many people, poor people mainly don't know a lot of things that there are in the world and because they don't know them, then they don't want them, and they don't dream about them and they don't fight for them and they don't try to transform the world in order to get them."

I'll close with a comment from another activist for development, educational psychologist Paul Carlin from Oslo. "My Vygotsky was an aloof, distant scientist, when I first met him at the university of Oslo. He was mostly used in theoretical dueling with the ghost of Piaget in student papers over casting development as blank slate or the preplanned blooming of biology. And the zones of proximal development were represented by technical drawings and equations on the blackboard. The drawings traced the predicted path/bridge within a ZPD of the transformation of a skill from novice to expert. My Vygotsky never questioned the tool-for-result methodology.

Big Ideas and Revolutionary Activity

Never imagined another ontology. What I really appreciate and in turn struggle with in implementing this revolutionary Vygotsky is that it opened my imagination to what is alive, transformable, buildable. A new psychology of becoming. That the human world is alive in a myriad of ways, not dead, commodified, closed off. Celebrate what has been built for us to build with further."

Blog Posts

In addition to Lois' chapters, articles and public talks we have offered in this book, we have included a selection of Lois' blog posts. Lois's blogs can be found at *Psychology Today* (https://www.psychologytoday.com/experts/lois-holzman-phd), and on her website, Loisholzman.org. In her blogs, Lois continues her discussions surrounding her concerns with the dualistic (and stigmatizing) nature of psychology, the overdetermined assumptions in philosophy that have skewed our understandings of what it means to learn, know and develop, as well as the harmful consequences that derive from the devaluation/absence of play in our educational system and beyond. Yet far from being discussions of despair, Lois' blog posts always offer a way forward by reminding us that as historical-sociocultural makers of meaning, we have the ability to transform our environments, ourselves and each other by reorganizing the determining circumstances in ways that better suit our collective needs. True to Vygotsky's activity-based tool-and-result methodology and her ongoing commitment to build a global community of performance activity-ists, Lois invites readers to continue the conversation by building with/upon her insights/offers and exploring where we might go next together.

Big Ideas and Revolutionary Activity

Activist-Scholars:
A Story within a Story

Posted on January 30, 2017

I want to introduce you to a unique activist-scholar community that played an especially important role in my development. It's the Laboratory of Comparative Human Cognition (also known as LCHC or, simply, the Lab). Housed at the University of California San Diego since 1979, the Lab is a community of interdisciplinary scholars who share an interest in the study of human mind in its cultural and historical contexts, and who seek to resolve theoretical and methodological problems associated with scholarly approaches that place culture and activity at the center of attempts to understand human nature, with a particular focus on the sources of, and solutions to, problems of social inequality.

About five years ago, Michael Cole, the founder of LCHC, approached me and several other former Lab members to collectively tell the LCHC story. It's not completed yet (and might never be), but the story in process is available to read. We call it "The Story of LCHC – An Unfinished Polyphonic Autobiography." And it begins like this:

This "wiki narrative" website is an effort to tell the long story of a research organization, LCHC, through a diversity of voices. These voices belong to the scholars, students, and researchers who helped to establish the lab in the early 1970s as well as those who contributed to it at various points during the last half century. We emphasize that this project is still in progress. Our autobiographical account brings us only up to the mid 1990s. From time to time as life allows, we will continue our re-collection of the past even as we create a future.

In addition to the detailed history of the Lab, the website contains separate pages for those of us who wrote the story, as well as dozens of people who called LCHC home, whether they were involved for decades or a few months.

I created my page on the LCHC *Unfinished Polyphonic Autobiography* site in 2012. The story I tell there is as unfinished as the Lab's story. But it does describe an important piece of my scholar-activist journey, one that I stick by nearly five years later. I hope you enjoy it!

My Story @ LCHC

I came to Rockefeller University and LCHC in the fall 1976 from Lois Bloom's lab at Teachers College Columbia University. I had just completed (but not yet defended) my PhD dissertation (in developmental psychology and psycholinguistics) on the development of the expression of causal relations in/by 2-3 year olds. It was a naturalistic, lon-

Big Ideas and Revolutionary Activity

gitudinal study of the relationship between thinking and speaking, and to some extent a critique of Piagetian genetic epistemology, with an ever so slight bow to Vygotsky's more social-cultural understanding. I had been involved in the ongoing Bloom lab project for several years, yielding 4-5 co-authored, data-driven published studies putting forth the beginnings of a methodology for the study of child language that was (in LCHC language) ecologically valid.

Prior to the Bloom lab, I had begun a PhD program in linguistics at Brown, where involvement in the new edition of DARE (Dictionary of American Regional English) sent me into the field (rural Rhode Island!), and a fellowship to teach English to foreign graduate students sent me into a tizzy of improvisation. Both piqued my interest in how to study/understand language as a human social activity and began to shape my skepticism toward mainstream social science methods. I transferred to Columbia's linguistics department in 1969 when faced with the choices of moving to NYC, La Jolla or Champaign-Urbana (due to job offers from psychology departments to my then-husband Don Hood), NYC was a no brainer. But it turned out that Columbia's linguistics department was not for me—at the time, child language was not considered a legitimate object of study. I switched to psychology and then developmental psychology in a search to find people and a place with similar interests to mine. But within linguistics at Columbia, I was introduced to Chomsky's formalism, Diver's odd behavioral structuralism, and Labov, and learned that there are many ways to look and that how you look shapes what you see!

I also taught high school English for a year between college and grad school in Smithfield RI, which was white working-class rural at the time. I mention it because discovering that many of the students had never even been to Providence, much less Boston, had a huge impact on me, and probably has something to do with my commitment to the All Stars Project's work and my belief in what Kwame Appiah calls cosmopolitanism and its role in ongoing development.

I suppose all this can be framed in terms of questions I brought to LCHC, like the following:

- can we study the activities of living social beings without distorting these activities;
- how can we come to understand/discover what language (e.g., speaking *how, when, why, with* and *for whom*) is and what it does in the world;
- how do human beings become language users and makers and how come some do it with ease and others with varying levels of difficulty;
- what's the relationship, if any, between doing language well and being smart;
- if language is not the mirror of thought, what is the relationship between the two;
- why don't I buy into existing theories of human development and are there other theories I don't know about;
- why do kids get turned off to schooling when they are so eager to learn.

I was at the Lab from 1976-79 and worked almost exclusively on what became known as "ecological validity" and the Manhattan Country School project, with Mike, Ray McDermott and Ken Trauppman. The lasting learnings from those years include:

- an understanding of the laboratory as an invalid methodology and the conundrum that this presents;
- the socio-cultural situatedness of learning and development;
- the contemporary potential of Vygotsky's work;
- the politics (both petty and not) of psychology and the social sciences;
- the creativity that comes from cross-fertilizing disciplines.

The overarching moral-political issue the Lab highlighted for me was the responsibility that psychology and the other social sciences have for perpetuating racism and poverty and their negative impacts on people's lives, and the challenges to those of us who work to overturn this.

At the same time as I joined the Lab I met Fred Newman, a philosopher turned community activist and creator/practitioner/trainer of a radical (in both the political and scientific-methodological senses) form of therapy, social therapy. Fred's critique of psychology had different intellectual origins from mine and other Lab members, and added a new and lasting dimension to my thinking. The similarities and differences between what he and his group were doing in trying to create a new psychology as part of community activism and what we at the Lab were trying to do excited me. I began working with Newman simultaneous with working at the Lab. It was an opportunity to participate in a socio-cultural experiment that was community-based and not reliant on organized funding sources (e.g., government or corporate funding or university affiliation) for its existence, which meant that creating its financial base was simultaneously a community-building activity.

Over the years, Newman, Lenora Fulani (who I met at the Lab and who joined our work around 1980) and I, and many others, created the East Side Institute, the Social Therapy centers around the country, the All Stars Project, Independent Voting.org (and other organizations that came and went). From the beginning, we believed that developing new conceptual frameworks, methodologies and practices required the simultaneous building of a fully participatory community and that these two tasks required an independent location, that is, one free of institutional ties to university, government, corporation or foundation. We later realized that this was an application of what Vygotsky referred to as the search for method, i.e., simultaneously, "tool-and-result."

I've been a key person in this socio-cultural experiment since 1976. Although I've been involved in all of its varied activities, most of my work emanates from the East Side Institute, which Newman and I founded in the 1980s, and from my affiliation with the All Stars Project, which Fulani and Newman founded. The Institute is a small non-profit organization dedicated to new approaches to human development, learning, therapeutics and community building. Our staff is comprised of volunteer

Big Ideas and Revolutionary Activity

professionals and interns, and our faculty is all volunteer. Our modest funding comes from a few hundred individuals. This independent location allows the Institute to be inclusive, to bring together people who do not ordinarily come together, and to do other things that would not be possible in a traditionally funded institution, e.g., accept people from all over the world into our programs without prerequisites or requirements; train nonprofessionals and professionals together; collaborate freely and with no strings attached; and act on research and program initiatives with a minimum of bureaucracy. This has been particularly important for psychology, social work and education professionals frustrated by their work in traditional institutions who come to us for a learning experience that is not acquisitional or evaluative, and a community that is not disciplinarily bounded.

Somewhere in the 1990s, we began to refer to our location/activity as "the development community" because it had grown substantially and was open to anyone who wanted to participate in building it/fostering human development. And because what we were/are doing in the areas of psychology, psychotherapy, education, politics and culture was/is relevant to academics, yet was/is created outside of academic institutions, I continuously bring our activities to academia and vice versa. This has always involved engaging some key questions and the challenge of finding academics willing to engage them with me! Institutional location matters. It raises questions about disciplinary and institutional boundaries and their impact on the production and dissemination of ideas: Where do they come from and how are they produced? How free is the intellectual marketplace? Does crossing its borders, as the Institute and I do, exacerbate them or begin to dissolve them? Social psychologist Ken Gergen places the Institute's work as outside what he calls "the tyranny of the normal—the patterns of expectations, obligations and swift sanctions within the core of most disciplines;" it is, to him, a place where it is possible to "risk innovation." Gergen's characterization seems apt to me. It raises some issues that I see as continuous with and at the same time extensions of the Lab's discoveries, insights, successes and failures.

For example, if social therapy groups are effective zones of emotional development, what are the implications for the institution of psychotherapy that the practice has been developed and flourishes outside psychology's professional and methodological borders? Could such a practice, in which people grow emotionally through engaging in the collective activity of breaking down psychology's methodological dualisms, be taught within academia and implemented widely in clinics? Could our work be helpful to those academics and practitioners who are fighting an uphill battle trying to change the medical model of therapeutic treatment? If not, what methodological and political issues does this raise for all of us?

And, if successful approaches to developing children (including their developing as successful learners) are being implemented outside of schools and independent of university think tanks, what does that say about the current organization of educational research? If performing onstage helps children and youth perform in life, shouldn't educators take a long hard look at their cognitive bias? Could the performatory and improvisational method of the All Stars and the Institute replace the behavior management approach taught in schools of education (and the methods of teaching teachers as well)? If segregating children into age or "ability" groups is shown to be socially, cognitively and emotionally detrimental, what does school reform mean? And if the All Stars youth programs have effected a unique kind of partnership with business leaders to support the development of inner city youth, what are the implications for philanthropy and educational research funding?

Choosing not to move with the Lab to UCSD in 1979, I took a faculty position at Empire State College, the "non-traditional" part of SUNY and was there until 1997. This proved invaluable in allowing me to experiment with creative, collective and performatory organizations of learning environments, something that my short stint as a high school teacher and the ecological validity work had shown were desperately needed. It also provided me with a legitimate (if not prestigious) academic location from which to continue to perform as an academic. My published work during the early Empire State College years continued to examine language and language development, although with a more political and philosophical critique than previously (e.g., 1982, "Growing up explained: Vygotskians look at the language of causality"; 1982, "The politics of autism: A socio-historical view"; 1985, "Pragmatism and dialectical materialism in language development,") and began to articulate the Vygotskian practice my colleagues and I were creating therapeutically through Newman's social therapy (e.g., 1979, *The Practice of Method*) and educationally through the establishment of the Barbara Taylor School (e.g., 1989, "Developing poor and minority children as leaders with the Barbara Taylor School Educational Model"). I also published, in 1990, "Lev and let Lev: An interview on the life and works of Lev Vygotsky" (with David Bakhurst, Guillermo Blanck, Mariane Hedegaard, David Joravsky, Christine LaCerva, Siebren Miedema, Luis Moll, and Jim Wertsch) in *Practice, The Magazine of Psychology and Political Economy*, an Institute journal from 1983-1991.

Over the years my work became increasingly multi-faceted—focusing on advancing/understanding social therapy through my Vygotskian and Fred's Wittgensteinian lens, transforming the Harlem-based Barbara Taylor School into an unorthodox Vygotskian laboratory, building ties with alternative educators and postmodern, humanistic and critical psychologists nationally and internationally, and "discovering" performance as a powerfully developmental form of play (and vice versa) at all ages—all the while doing grassroots organizing in the poor communities.

When we began what is now the All Stars Project in 1983, it was as a response to welfare mothers in NYC we were organizing, who asked us to give their kids something to do. We asked the kids what they wanted to do and they said, "Have a talent show." So we did, in a Bronx church basement. And we organized young people and adults to put on another. And another. We launched the All Stars Talent Show Network around the City. We set up a non-profit and went door to door and stood on street corners to raise money for it. At the time, we billed it as "an anti-violence program where kids did something positive for their community." It grew. We saw how powerful perform-

Big Ideas and Revolutionary Activity

ing on stage was for the kids and their families and how it moved the adult supporters. We saw kids building their organization and growing from it. We saw our message that you can perform not just on stage but in life become a reality. We realized the program was a development program, in which kids were performing their development with each other, with adults, with their families and community.

Other All Stars youth programs were launched, and partnerships with business leaders (of varied political persuasions) and performance artists flourished, all around the activity of performance on and off stage being a developmental experience. The All Stars currently works with 10,000 young people yearly in NYC, Newark NJ, San Francisco and Chicago (with a 2010 launch in Uganda and several other countries in beginning stages of development). 2013 was a year of growth for the All Stars, with the opening of a state of the art center in Newark's downtown arts district, complete with the country's first Institute for Afterschool Development, and a center in Dallas due to open in the fall.

Off the official academic radar in its early decades, the All Stars is increasingly known to academics and policy makers, who find the longevity and success of both its youth development model and its ability to raise private funding (currently over $7 million yearly) harder and harder to ignore. In the last few years, All Stars' founders Fulani and Newman and President and CEO Gabrielle Kurlander have issued white papers addressing the education crisis in America, essays that directly challenge the "achievement gap" framing of the issue (2010, Achievement Gap or Development Gap?) and put forth the provocation that if we all (kids, teachers, parents and other adults) pretended that underachieving kids were good learners they would become so (2011, Let's Pretend). Fulani's latest (2013) is The Development Line: Helping the Poor to Grow—A Special Report on Solving the Poverty Crisis in America.

LCHC's insistence on the unit of analysis being "the person-environment interface" and its budding realization of Vygotsky's dialectical methodology for studying/producing ongoing human development and learning informed all that Newman, Fulani and I have done. The interplay of our interventions/organizing activity and our theorizing were (and remain), in some ways, a continuation of grappling with issues expressed in different terms at Rockefeller University: how the dominant understandings of the relationship between development and learning, language and thought, cognition and emotion, work and play, and individual and group are played out in the lives of people, with tragically non-developmental consequences for them and the world.

In 1991 Valerie Walkerdine (who I met at LCHC when she was a visiting scholar) asked Newman and me to write a book on Vygotsky for Routledge's Critical Psychology series she was co-editor of. *Lev Vygotsky: Revolutionary Scientist* came out in 1993, the first of three books Newman and I would co-author over a five year period. *Revolutionary Scientist* was unique in several ways. It presented Vygotsky as a Marxist methodologist, both locating him in his historical period and delineating how his life and writings have been a catalyst for a contemporary revolutionary, practical-critical, psychology. It highlighted Vygotsky's unconventional view of how development and learning are related and, in doing so, brought human development into prominence. It introduced important linkages between Vygotsky's views on thinking and speaking and those of Wittgenstein, drawing implications for language acquisition and language learning. And it drew attention to Vygotsky's understanding of the role of play in child development, and expanded on the significance of play throughout the lifespan. In these ways, this classic text presented a more expansive Vygotsky than previously understood. In 2013, the book was reissued as a Psychology Press Classic Edition in Psychology, with a new introduction.

Unscientific Psychology and *The End of Knowing* explicate in more detail our critique of mainstream psychology, the Marxian, Wittgensteinian and Vygotskian contributions to our critique and practice (in Marx's words, our "practical-critical activity"), and our growing postmodern interest and sentiment. These books helped spread our ideas internationally and lay the foundation for a series of international conferences, training programs and partnerships the Institute initiated in 1997. But before then, we engaged with the Russian Vygotskians at Eureka (the first post-Soviet university from which Elina Lampert-Shepel comes), developed a close relationship with Gita Vygoskaya, Elena Kravtsova and Gennady Kravtsov and kept working to articulate our understanding of the importance of Vygotsky's tool-and-result methodology, his discovery of "completion" and the implications of his brief writings on play to anyone who would listen. Our Barbara Taylor School--a twelve-year experiment in radical education, 1985-1997, failed as a viable enterprise but it was a hotbed of discovery about the above, brought us many interested visitors, and helped to establish me as a legitimate "Vygotskian" (among some). I wrote several articles and the book *Schools for Growth: Radical Alternatives to Current Educational Models* about this work. *Schools* also looks at the Russian Golden Key School and the Sudbury Valley School alternative learning environments.

And performance? It entered our work from many directions: from Vygotsky's insight that play is how/where/when the child is as if "a head taller;" from Newman beginning to write and direct plays and the improv comedy troupe he began; from leading performance workshops for non-performers as a social therapeutic experiment; from my looking at social therapy groups as the creating of ZPDs simultaneous with the creating of new emotionality; from our developing a street performance ensemble method of fundraising for the All Stars Project; from collaborative work with Ken Gergen and our mutual interest in developing what we termed performative psychology and bringing it into APA and other mainstream venues. Among my attempts to share this history, articulate the methodology and describe the practice are my 2009 book *Vygotsky at Work and Play* and the essay "Performing a Life (Story)."

By 1997 Newman and I were in rich dialogue not only with Gergen but also with others who were developing and/or articulating cultural and historical ways of understanding and studying human life, including Mary Gergen, John Shotter, Ian Parker, Erica Burman, Sheila McNamee and John Morss. We decided to host an international

Big Ideas and Revolutionary Activity

conference, which we called "Unscientific Psychology: Conversations with Other Voices." About 200 people attended and joined us in what was part academic conference with lectures by each of the above (subsequently published as *Postmodern Psychologies, Societal Practice and Political Life*) and part improvisational performance of a play created out of participants' "performances of their lives." Unscientific Psychology was many things— an indication of interest in postmodern and cultural psychology from many corners of the world, an experiment in an alternative mode of playing with ideas and sharing work across disciplines and approaches, and a testing ground for the Institute's approach to group creativity.

In 2001, we partnered again with Gergen to hold the first Performing the World (PTW) conference. In October 2012, the Institute and the All Stars Project hosted the seventh. Over the decade the use of performance, play, and the creative and expressive arts as a tool in social change, community-building and educational work has grown rapidly, and more and more practitioners and scholars are being won over from an instrumental view of performance to performance being how human beings develop and learn. PTW is both tool-and-result of this motion, a practical critique of mainstream social science, education, therapy and humanitarian work, and a needed support network and community for those doing this kind of work that is considered on the fringe.

My involvement in international organizing/learning/teaching also includes several international programs and activities I've launched that link scholars, practitioners, educators, artists and social change activists who have a performance/creativity/play bent. It's a challenge and privilege to work with psychologists, community theatre people, grassroots activists and youth workers from China, India, Bangladesh, Japan, Mexico, Nicaragua, Serbia, Brazil, Uganda, etc., many of whom work with the most marginalized and poor people, side by side with Americans and Western Europeans. It's this activity, more than any other I'm involved in day-to-day, in which practical-critical politics, philosophy and psychology are most fused. It's also the most moving part of all my work, because it directly touches world poverty.

My most recent writings and academic activities involve speaking within and across disciplines and traditions: about the postmodernizing of Marxism to Marxists (e.g., 2003, "All Power to the Developing;" 2011, Fred Newman and the *Practice of Method*), what activity theory brings to postmodernism and vice versa (e.g., 2006, "Activating Postmodernism."), how philosophers of language and science are among the most rigorous of critical psychologists (e.g., 2011, "Critical Psychology, Philosophy and Social Therapy"), what outside of school practices tell us about learning in school, how therapy and theatre can create culture rather than merely replicate it, and the historical imperative of the shift to the performatory in all areas of human life.

Play, performance, group creativity, the insidiousness of boundaries, pain, suffering and massive underdevelopment, a belief in continuous developmental (revolutionary) activity, organizing environments for people (kids especially) to create more options for themselves for how to be in the world and change it…this is what brought me back to LCHC. And our individual and collective staying power.

Play as if Your Mental Health Depended on It

Play helps us move around depression, anxiety, hopelessness and loneliness.

Posted November 2, 2016

I don't like labels, so one of the things I play around with is what to call myself. I used to say I'm a developmental psychologist, since that's what I was trained to be. But developmental psychology is an academic discipline that studies people and explains them in ways I have some big problems with. So I started to call myself a developmentalist to highlight that I try to help people develop and grow. I also sometimes say I'm an activity-ist since it's human activity and not behavior that I am interested in and want to foster. Lately I've been saying I'm a play revolutionary. Now you might find it strange to put those two words together. But they're more similar than you think. Both play and revolution transform what is into something qualitatively different. As a play revolutionary, I believe that play can revolutionarily transform the world and all of its people.

Until recently if I had to come up with an opposite of play I would say it's what learning has become in our rigid, structured, test-driven elementary, middle and high school classrooms. There's no play there. Even at the university level, play tends to be separated out into sports and the theatre department.

Growing up socialized to a world divided in this way, no matter our age, we're deprived of the emotional, social and intellectual growth that play provides us in all areas of our lives. In the past decade, this deprivation has reached epidemic proportions in the U.S. and many other highly industrialized countries. Anthropologist and pioneer play researcher Brian Sutton-Smith spoke to the depth of the deprivation of play when he wrote, *"The opposite of play is not a present reality or work. It is depression."*

This is especially serious when so many experts are telling us there's an epidemic of depression in the US across the lifespan. Depression, along with anxiety, hopelessness and loneliness are the most frequent feelings college students report, according to about a dozen national surveys done by associations of university and college counseling centers, college health services, and the American Psychological Association. And the number has risen dramatically in the last ten years—with 35-45% of college students currently reporting these as reasons they sought help.

Big Ideas and Revolutionary Activity

Play helps us move about and around depression, anxiety, hopelessness and loneliness. *Play doesn't merely change us; it transforms us.* Change adds or subtracts—it has to do with quantity. Transformation "changes everything"—it has to do with quality. It makes what is into something qualitatively new.

I'm writing this and you're reading it because we played our way into becoming who we are today. Way back when, we were babbling, crawling little babies. Way back when, we played—and it changed everything. We played at speaking and walking before we knew how to speak or walk, and that's how come we became speakers and walkers. Our caregivers helped us (they played right along with us) and they absolutely loved us for it and cheered us on. They helped us play at being "bigger" and older and more skilled than we actually were—or as one of my heroes, the early 20th century psychologist Lev Vygotsky, says —as if we are "a head taller" than we are.

This phrase— "a head taller"—captures how and why human beings develop and learn—because we are not only who are at any given moment or age or stage of life. We are also other than who we are. We are simultaneously who we are *and* who we are becoming. We are babies who can't speak a language *and*—through play—we are speakers.

This playful way of being in the world with others is something that all of us, at any age, can do. But most of us stop. It's not our fault. A bias against play is deep in our culture. We're taught that play is frivolous. That there's a difference between learning and playing—and that learning is what matters. We're told constantly who we are — and that limits who we can become. We focus on getting it right and looking good— and that stops us from developing. Without play, we get stuck. Individuals get stuck. Families get stuck. Communities get stuck. Nations get stuck. Indeed, these days the whole world appears stuck in old roles, stale performances, destructive games, and emotional turmoil.

Being stuck is standing still. To get unstuck, we have to move. And play is *movement*. In physical space, in time, *and* in the always becoming-ness of our lives. When we move, we get a new perspective. Turn your head 90 degrees and what you see is different from what you saw seconds ago. Walk your usual running path and you'll have a new perspective. Strike a power pose as you walk into a job interview and you'll feel different about the conversation you're about to have. Walk into your house or office backwards and you'll see it in a new way. Try dancing with your partner or housemates when you get home instead of mumbling hello. When we play with how we do familiar things, we discover what's always been there. We create new ways to feel, new ideas and new beliefs. We discover *and* create what we're made of.

Play gives us permission to be other than who we are in "real life." It allows us to imagine ourselves as being, feeling and doing different. Just as little children pretend to be fantastical characters or Mommy and Daddy, and older ones imagine themselves into basketball or tennis greats and the next Beyoncé or Adele, we adults can and should create ways of playing that require us to step out of our usual roles and identities. To move about and around those roles and identities.

Play gives us permission to "cheat"—to creatively imitate those more skilled than we are at something. Babies don't become speakers by studying a grammar book or dictionary. They play with words and sounds. They imitate others. The same for the rest of us—whether you're beginning to sing, learning to cook, speaking in public, or becoming a parent. We play at being others. We do what we see them doing (hopefully with their help and encouragement). But since it's US doing it and not them, it becomes uniquely ours and we become singers and chefs and public speakers and parents.

Play helps us belong. Belonging helps us move about and around feeling alone, isolated and victimized. Playing is how we become part of existing communities—the human community, first and foremost, and the thousands of communities, large and small, that humans create. Think of the communities you've become part of through transforming yourself into a member of that community, by imagining yourself as a competent member and creatively imitating others, in other words, by playing at being a member before you knew how.

Play is also how we create new communities. There's something very special about belonging to a community or a group that you were part of creating, that didn't exist before, that got built through you and others working and playing together. You not only have the community, but you also have new kinds of relationships with your fellow builders, relationships nurtured and supported by the very community you built!

As a play revolutionary I invite people to play with anything and everything in their lives. That's because for me *play is more about the how than the what*. Play has to do with how we do the things we do. It generates choices: you can go to work, hang out with friends, do chores, study, have an argument, and so on, in the way you typically do (as who you "are") or you can engage in these life activities playfully, that is, inviting the transformative movement of becoming-ness.

Big Ideas and Revolutionary Activity

"We're Not Buying It!"

Survey on Emotional Distress and Diagnosis Reveals Mistrust of Psychiatric Labeling

Posted July 14, 2016

It's been a little over one year since the Survey on Emotional Distress and Mental Health Diagnosis was launched online.

The survey was designed by the East Side Institute, an organization with a long-standing opposition to the individualized model of human development and the medicalized understanding of emotionality.

Very few public opinion polls on mental health issues have been conducted, and those that do exist are "forced choice" and presuppose an illness model. We at the East Side Institute wanted people to get the opportunity to reflect on and socialize their thoughts about the medical-mental illness-diagnostic model and its impact on their lives. And that is what they did! We have results from over 1000 surveys—mostly from across the US, but 33 other countries are also represented—and they're quite revealing. Despite being bombarded with medical-mental illness-diagnostic propaganda, people are skeptical of the model. Their concerns ranged from pragmatic to ethical, from philosophical to political.

I recently completed a draft paper summarizing and discussing the survey results for a special issue of a journal dedicated to the growing movement to develop alternatives to the current diagnostic system in psychiatry and clinical psychology. Here's a sneak preview of what a thousand people told us. (Lesson: if you ask people to tell you what they think—*without telling them how they should think*—they'll tell you!).

- Despite the fact that emotional distress is presented as diagnosable illness by nearly every institution and professional people have contact with, most of them are not buying it. At best, diagnosis is a necessary evil, required under the current system in order to have the possibility of getting some help. At worst, it is stigmatizing, limiting of possibilities, isolating and potentially physically harmful.

- There was significant awareness of the corruption of mental health services by pharmaceutical companies and, more broadly, the politics of a medicalized mental health system.

- The idea that emotional distress is caused by chemical imbalance or brain disorder was soundly rejected. The popularization of neuroscience research seems bogus to some and to others a denial of mind-body holism and human relationality. Neither view dampers the interest people have in the notion that the brain plays a role in our emotionality.

Big Ideas and Revolutionary Activity

- Sociality and mind-body unity were also apparent in the responses to how to help people in emotional distress. Talking to people, being listened to, and therapy were most frequent. Social activities of many kinds, as well as yoga and meditation, were also common responses.

- There was an understanding of and appreciation for the impact of diagnosis on mental health professionals. Some people were critical and some were sympathetic of the predicament professionals face—having to work with a model that distorts the people in front of you and is impossible to "get right" but, nevertheless, being influenced to see and relate to people in terms of that model.

- People encouraged more surveys and conversations like these. Forty-eight percent of survey takers asked to be contacted for further conversation.

- People were appreciative of being included in the ongoing debate over diagnosis and alternatives to it. They wanted their voices heard—with 87% of survey takers having something to tell the professionals directly.

Holiday Warning: Giving Can Change Your Life!

Some counter-intuitive thoughts about gifts, giving, receiving and therapy.

Posted December 15, 2014

During this holiday season it's appropriate to share some thoughts on giving and getting. I live in NYC and during these weeks the streets and avenues, stores and outdoor markets are even more crowded than usual—jammed, really—with people shopping. It is, indeed, the "giving" season. The giving is, of course, orchestrated by retailers and their parent companies and the media. The pressure to make your lists, figure your budget (and no doubt spend over it) is very, very strong. I personally don't participate in it, preferring to give gifts at any time of the year when it feels right. And yet, my friends and relatives who do participate in the holiday tell me that they greatly enjoy the activity of giving to their loved ones at this time of year. I hope that even the most frenzied and the most economically strapped among us feel good about giving.

But psychologically speaking, there's a lot more to be gained from being giving to others. And each of us has a whole lot more to give than a gift you bought or made for someone this holiday season or some other special occasion. It turns out that giving is psychologically healthy. It can help us grow emotionally and socially—at any age.

I learned this from the philosopher-therapist Fred Newman. Newman believed that giving was an active sharing of whatever we have, rather than a ritualized transaction. For him, this includes sharing what we think of as "our emotional possessions"— our pathology, our pain and our humiliation.

Newman learned this from his group therapy practice. He saw how hard it was for clients, *especially* when they were in emotional pain or crisis, to give and let others give to them. But when they did, it was emotionally transformative, not only for them but for their entire therapy group. People *felt* differently and spoke with each other in new ways. A hallmark of Newman's therapy, social therapy, is to support people to give their emotionality to others and to help them learn to let others give to them.

Newman was a social critic whose understanding of how society and culture shape our emotionality informed his practice. His belief in the developmental power of giving was informed by his analysis of the kind of world we are socialized to. To Newman, we live in a "culture of getting." In his book, *Let's Develop! A Guide to Continuous Personal Growth* (written with Phyllis Goldberg), he devotes an entire

Big Ideas and Revolutionary Activity

chapter to "Giving in a Culture of Getting." Here he describes the getting culture and how it keeps us emotionally underdeveloped, and he shows how we can all get emotionally smarter if we organize our lives around giving. In other words, even while living in a non-developmental culture of getting, we can still develop by creating our own "subversive" giving culture.

Newman begins the chapter this way:

> Whether or not we believe in the abstract that it's more blessed to give than to receive, in our everyday lives most of us are practitioners (more or less successful) of getting. Getting is not only a totally legitimate activity in our culture, it's highly valued. People who are good at getting (the go-getters) are admired and rewarded. Those who aren't often become objects of pity or blame; they don't 'get it,' they're losers, unhip, failures.

> We are trained from early childhood to play the getting game. The object of the game is to get as much as you can while giving as little as you can. Although you can't expect to get something for nothing, the rules of the game say that you give only in order to get. Giving more than you get, or giving anything away if you can get something for it, is a sign of poor judgment—or worse.

And why give? Because, according to Newman, in such a culture we are actually helped more by giving than we are by getting. Always playing by the rules of the getting culture can leave us socially deprived and emotionally limited. He described his practice this way:

> The social therapeutic approach helps people to break out of the getting mode, to put aside the getting principle (where appropriate) in favor of a more sophisticated and gratifying method for living.

When people manage to do so, it is usually and not surprisingly, with great conflict.

> ...being unusually giving violates a fundamental principle of our culture. So people tend to worry that they'll be ripped off. In our culture of getting, people are getting ripped off, emotionally speaking and otherwise, much of the time. Paradoxically, it's only when you're unconditionally giving emotionally that you can't get ripped off at all. (Someone named Jesus said that!) What's more, the more you give, the less time you have to spend and the less mental energy you have to exert worrying that you'll be ripped off or resenting that you have been. What a relief!

Becoming a giver in a culture of getting is, among other things, a wonderful process of discovering something about yourself.

> How do people who have been socialized in the culture of getting come to see themselves as having something to give? *By giving. They give, and in doing so they discover that they have something to give—not the other way around.*

Our emotional health as individuals and a culture could be greatly enhanced if "that most wonderful time of the year" could go on for 12 months.

Big Ideas and Revolutionary Activity

Why Ask Why?

Sometimes We Just Need to Move On.

Posted October 8, 2014

Why is the sky blue? Why does snow melt? Why do people die? Why is that man sleeping on the street? Why can't I have ice cream? Why do I have to go to bed?

Young children are full of questions like these. They've learned from us that people ask why. As philosopher Ludwig Wittgenstein would say, they've learned to play a language game (a "form of life" or activity that human beings engage in), and through playing this particular language game over and over and over, they come to see and experience things and events causally and to expect that everything they encounter in the world is either the cause or the effect of something else.

At first, parents delight in the "wondering whys" ("Why is the sky blue?"), proud of their child's intelligence and curiosity. Sooner or later, though, most parents will tire of their children's barrage of questions (many or most of which they have no clue how to answer). And then there are the "whiney whys" ("Why can't I...?") which adults like even less. That's a different language game—whose next move is often one of the parental standbys, "Because," or, "Because I said so."

Once we're adults, "Why?" stays with us.

Causality is one of the ways we know—to know something has come to mean to know its causes and its effects. Causality, reality, and others are among the 12 categories of thought identified by 18th-century German philosopher Immanuel Kant to correspond to forms of understanding that are the foundations of our conceptual knowledge. These categorical ways of thinking are a priori, meaning they are independent of experience—they're the innate structures of the human mind. It's these categories, the story goes, that then shape our experiences. The short version, in the vernacular of our day, is, "We're programmed that way."

Traditional psychotherapy depends on causality. The working assumption is that identifying what is causing depression or anger or whatever—the cause usually being something in one's childhood—changes it, clears things up, and even makes a person better. I've long believed that the assumption of a causal relationship between past events and current emotions needs to be carefully examined—after all, it's the very foundation of a profession (and the industry it feeds) dedicated to helping people who are experiencing emotional distress.

There are at least two downsides to causality remaining unexamined:

Big Ideas and Revolutionary Activity

Ignoring the topic keeps valuable information away from both consumers and professionals. If conversations about mental health don't address the assumption of cause and why we should try to uncover it, then it's unlikely that the "helpers" and the "helped" will have opportunities to learn about the many available non-causal treatment options. None of us should be limited that way.

We lose the chance to look at ourselves and our own assumptions. Examining our assumptions is an important, often eye-opening and transformative experience. In the case of causality, when we do look, we see how obsessed we are with cause in everyday life. Do you know people who truly believe that every single thing and event has some other thing or event that caused it to be, and who won't rest until they believe they've pinpointed it? I do. Are you sometimes even more concerned with the cause of something—say, why a friend seemed to ignore you, or why you got angry at the cashier at the supermarket—than with ways to move on with your relationships and your life? Or maybe you think you can't take a course of action until you know why it happened in the first place.

I'm among quite a few psychologists who believe that, far from being the solution, trying to find the cause of feeling a certain way only exacerbates feeling that way—and that we need to loosen the hold causality has on us. Applying causality to the psychological realm, and insisting that all of human thought and action is best understood in terms of cause and effect, is misguided.

While mainstream therapy (of both the talk and drug variety) reinforces a causal view of the world, to those of us who practice non-causal approaches it is clear that much of people's emotional pain comes from thinking causally—and we're finding more and more evidence that challenging this way of thinking can be extremely helpful to people.

Here is a classic, hypothetical example:
- *Client*: I stayed in bed all day because I was depressed.
- *Therapist*: How do you know that? Maybe you were depressed because you stayed in bed all day. Or maybe one thing has nothing to do with the other.

By suggesting other ways of looking at the situation, the therapist opens the possibility for a new kind of therapeutic conversation—more a creative journey they will take together than a telling of information so the therapist can come up with the correct cause-effect explanation.

You can read more in Chapter 4, "The What and How of Knowing," from *The Overweight Brain: How Our Obsession with Knowing Keeps Us from Getting Smart Enough to Make a Better World*. And to learn more about the problems with thinking and speaking causally, and to find out about therapeutic approaches that don't, see *Philosophical Investigations: A Clinician's Guide to Social Therapy*, a book I co-edited with Dr. Rafael Mendez, and *Let's Develop! A Guide to Continuous Personal Growth* by Dr. Fred Newman.

Danger! A Frightening New Mental Illness

If you doubt the danger of diagnosis, you might have sluggish cognitive tempo.

Posted April 12, 2014

A friend from South Africa contacted me today to see if I had read the article about a new diagnosis, sluggish cognitive tempo. I hadn't. My first thought was that she must be referring to some parody of diagnosis in *The Onion*. But I followed her link and it was to *The New York Times*. What I found truly frightened me. This was no parody.

Even as ADHD diagnosis and medication is finally getting serious critical investigation, reporter Alan Schwarz tell us that "some powerful figures in mental health are claiming to have identified a new disorder that could vastly expand the ranks of young people treated for attention problems. Called sluggish cognitive tempo, the condition is said to be characterized by lethargy, daydreaming and slow mental processing. By some researchers' estimates, it is present in perhaps two million children. Experts pushing for more research into sluggish cognitive tempo say it is gaining momentum toward recognition as a legitimate disorder—and, as such, a candidate for pharmacological treatment."

It seems to me that it's time to stop identifying such people as "experts in mental health." They have nothing whatsoever to do with health. Their business is illness. They're illness makers. What they do is create illness—not merely mental (whatever that is supposed to mean) but social, cultural, political and ethical illness.

I don't know how else to describe what is being done by illness characterizations such as this one offered by one of Schwarz' experts:

> These children are not the ones giving adults much trouble, so they're easy to miss," Dr. McBurnett said. "They're the daydreamy ones, the ones with work that's not turned in, leaving names off of papers or skipping questions, things like that, that impinge on grades or performance. So anything we can do to understand what's going on with these kids is a good thing.

(Another expert recommends caution because "we haven't even agreed on the symptom list"—rather revealing about how this so-called science works: make up an illness and then claim to have found evidence for its existence in some of the things people do; then sell a drug that stops people from doing those things). Note above the 'it goes without saying' comment that it "is gaining momentum toward recognition as a

Big Ideas and Revolutionary Activity

legitimate disorder—and, as such, a candidate for pharmacological treatment."

What are we doing to our children—and, consequently, to everyone? How have we let an illness model transform what childhood—and, consequently, family life is? How has understanding "what's going on with these kids" (if, indeed, anything is going on with them) become identical to diagnosing them as sick?

But I'm not blaming them. We all share responsibility. I've been writing and speaking for quite a while here and elsewhere about our society's need to take a hard look at how we have a diagnostic way of life and what it's doing to us. During the DSM-5 controversy there were thousands of professionals and non-professionals who spoke out about both the silliness and the dangerousness of calling bereavement and forgetfulness illnesses. I am sure they will do the same with sluggish cognitive tempo. But I fear that without addressing and transforming the pervasive and more pernicious diagnostic way of seeing the world that we've all been socialized to—we'll soon have to daydream in secret, until we no longer have anything to daydream about.

The Surprising Secret of Why Therapy Works

Why does talking together make us feel better?

Posted November 21, 2013

The late psychotherapist Fred Newman was no friend of the individualistic and medical model approach to emotional pain. The creator of social therapy, a group non-diagnostic approach, Fred was also a philosopher. During the nearly 40 years during which he maintained a large group practice and trained and supervised hundreds of social workers, counselors, psychologists and psychiatrists in social therapy, he shared with people how they had helped him figure out the conundrum of therapy and discover its value and the source of the joy it gave him.

For a long time, Fred was stumped by how come therapy was effective in helping people deal with their emotional pain. He was philosophically "anti-therapy"—convinced that the inner-outer and self-other dichotomies that traditional therapy is based on were mistaken. Yet, when he himself went into therapy he found it invaluable. During that time and for all the years after when he was practicing, he never changed his belief about the mistaken paradigm. And he also never gave up his quest. He thought that if we could discover the secret of therapy's effectiveness, then maybe everyone could do it, maybe we could all be therapeutic with each other.

It was during the early 1990s that the puzzle was finally solved. The understandings of language, especially how speaking is socially completive of our thoughts, that are the hallmarks of Lev Vygotsky's and Ludwig Wittgenstein's writings, helped. Therapy is helpful because and to the extent that it socializes what we mistakenly experience as individualistic and private. It works because of what therapists and clients are doing together—not because of the therapist's expertise in fixing clients' faulty thinking processes, in interpreting or re-interpreting their life experiences, or in teaching them behavioral options. And what therapists and clients are doing together is creating something new—a new relationship, a new way of speaking, new meanings. This is possible because we are social beings who, in spite of the myth of individualism and inner states of mind, are forever interconnected in the activity of living. Therapy works because it exposes and creates with our relational interconnectivity. It "brings out" and develops what's most positive about us. The best therapy, Fred believed, helped people be nicer.

In a public lecture he delivered in 1998 in New York City, entitled "Therapeutics as a Way of Life," Fred said, "The process of therapy has nothing to do with any kind of internal mental surgery. I think that in the process of therapy, what happens is that we reshape community, we reshape our lives. Therapy has to do with helping people

Big Ideas and Revolutionary Activity

to be more giving, to grow, to learn, to be more responsive to environments, to learn how to interrelate and to recreate our humanness."

"Therapeutics as a way of life" has caught on in the fifteen years since. Bringing out what's best about what goes on in therapy rooms—the new kinds of conversations that get created, the intensified responsiveness to the other, the growth in relationship that occurs—is happening in other spaces and places. I see it in educational settings where kids are given responsibility for creating their learning environment, in consulting firms that are turning away from Power Point-presented rules and techniques and toward listening and relationship-building experiences, in psychotherapy trainings and conferences in which the topic is not the self but the other, in community-based organizations that don't just bring together people who are estranged or strangers to each other and hope for the best but engage with them in transforming their relationships.

People, especially those in emotional pain, don't need fixing. They need to grow. Psychology needs to be transformed. A new understanding and practice of human life needs to be created in which we are "therapeutic" with each other all the time.

A New Way of Seeing Development (Hint: We Make It Happen)

All the world's a stage—and we create the play.

Posted September 21, 2013

What does your mind's eye conjure up when hearing or seeing the phrase "stages of development"? A stepladder or a theater? For most people, it's a ladder or other step-like image. And why not? From Freud, Piaget and Erikson to today's popular experts on human development, we've been told that the human life process is a series of progressively higher stages that people pass through.

But I have a different picture. Along with many, many others—including psychologists, therapists, educators and parents—I see a theatrical stage instead. Inspired by Lev Vygotsky's social-cultural psychology, we believe development doesn't happens *to* us, but that we actively create it. *How* we create it is by creating stages on which we can perform our growth. In this framework, developmental stages are like performance spaces that we can set up at home, school, the workplace—anywhere.

This idea of performance spaces opens us up to seeing environment in new ways. In the words of the great philosopher, Ludwig Wittgenstein, it can free us from "the picture that held us captive." For environment, that captivating picture is a place, location, background or context in which things happen—the things that "impact on" us and our development. And what we get with this picture is a certain kind of developmental research revealing that certain "environmental factors" accelerate and others retard the normal process of development. We're told that homes filled with books foster early literacy development. That growing up in an abusive environment is a good predictor of whether a child will be overly aggressive or violent. That talking a lot to infants is critical for later enriched cognitive development. This conventional understanding of environment and the research that follows from it supports the belief that development happens *to* us.

But what if, instead, our development is created *by* us? Then so are our environments created by us. Environments become the performance spaces or "stages" that people create, shape and reshape together—not separate from, or prior to, or added on to living our lives and growing and changing, but right alongside and as part of it.

Books as environmental factors or context do little. Books as props in performance stages *created* by parents and babies do a lot!

Big Ideas and Revolutionary Activity

To learn more about the new way of seeing "stages of development" and how it is helping people learn and grow, see *Vygotsky at Work and Play* and *Schools for Growth: Radical Alternatives to Current Educational Models*. And try it out for yourself.

The Biggest Myths About Emotions & How to Weaken Their Grip

Where do emotions live? The answer may surprise you.

Posted September 12, 2013

With all the chatter about emotions and the brain, you might think that neuroscience is the only exciting frontier in the study of human emotionality. You'd be wrong, though.

Just as busy are the social psychologists, the relational therapists, and the postmodern and the CHAT (Cultural Historical Activity Theorists). As one of them, I can share some of the latest thinking about our emotional lives. A lot of it goes against the dominant view and while I won't shatter the major myths about emotion that run rampant, I might at least weaken them a bit.

Emotions are an activity, a form of life. If they're "located" anywhere, they're in the world, not in our heads.

Emotions are culturally and socially produced and created. Their meaning is in how they're being responded to by others and by ourselves—both in the moment and in the ongoing cultural and social history of emotions.

The expression "form of life" comes from the philosopher Ludwig Wittgenstein. He was countering the "obsession" philosophers and scientists have for consistency, for having things fit together, correspond to one another, and be causally connected—leading them down the dark hole of reductionism from which there was no escape. Here's an excerpt from Wittgenstein's writings I especially like. It's not about emotions per se, but it makes his point rather well and shows his unique style of writing in numbered paragraphs. (I think every therapist should try reading Wittgenstein).

> I saw this man years ago: now I have seen him again, I recognize him, I remember his name. And why does there have to be a cause of this remembering in my nervous system? Why must something or other, whatever it may be, be stored-up there in any form? Why must a trace have been left behind? Why should there not be a psychological regularity to which no physiological regularity corresponds? If this upsets our concepts of causality then it is high time they were upset. (from Wittgenstein's Zelig, paragraph 905)

There are neurological and cognitive processes going on whenever we do anything, so of course they're going on whenever we recognize, remember and are emotional. But it doesn't follow that these processes are causally connected to or correspond

Big Ideas and Revolutionary Activity

to *what* we're recognizing, remembering or being emotional about, or to *human activity* of recognizing, remembering or being emotional.

Emotions aren't things we have or possess. They're things we *do*. Some of us cultural and postmodern oriented psychologists make emotions actions. We see and study how people "perform emotions" and "create emotional scenarios." We prefer these active, theatrical terms to the usual static noun that abandons emotionality's socialness and relationality and, with it, its meaning.

We can—and do—create new emotional forms of life.
We don't have a fixed or finite number of emotions.

Many experts believe that emotions should and can be defined and classified. They come up with the "basic" emotions (usually 6 or 8, including fear, happiness, anger, joy, etc). and then create lists of dozens of combinations of these basic ones. They hold to an "essentialist" view that emotions are, well, emotions—no matter when and where you live or who you are. But for those of us who disagree, that makes no sense. If everything about our lives is different today from a hundred years ago, our emotional lives are different. If my life is nothing life a twelve year-old Syrian boy's life, how can our anger be the same? What goes on in our brains might be the same but in no way does that mean our anger is the same.

Whatever you think of emoticons, the hundreds available—with more appearing every week—suggests that people (at least those who use social media) aren't limiting themselves to the "6 (or 8) human emotions," but are playing with ways to share their rich emotional forms of life in entirely new ways. Who knows, maybe this kind of play is enriching their emotional lives.

Performing—A New Way to Live

To be alive is to perform and play, so say psychology and theatre innovators.

Posted July 23, 2013

As a developmental psychologist, I have to keep up with discoveries and emerging movements in a host of fields outside of psychology—after all, human development is emotional, cultural, political, economic, and much more. I've learned so much from people in the theatre, especially those who practice and theorize performance.

For about a decade or so, people all over the world have been discovering each other as part of a global movement for "performance activism." What's meant by that term is that what it means to be alive is to perform and play, and that making a better world needs to involve people in creating new performances of ourselves (new "plays") because how we're currently performing—as a species—is, well, pretty horrific.

I'm one of many in the social sciences, education, medicine and theater who are involving all kinds of people in creating community projects, programs and organizations that support adults and children to create new performances of ourselves, both on stage and off. I also speak to the academic world about performance as a critically important but overlooked topic of study in psychology, about how our ability to be who we are and other than who we are *at the same time* is what learning and developing are all about. And I experience an enormous desire on the part of students and scholars, and lay people alike, for this new hopeful, "radically humanistic" way of seeing and relating to people as active performers of development and change.

One of the innovators I've learned a lot from is Richard Schechner. Richard is a professor at New York University's Tisch School of the Arts and the founder of the field know as Performance Studies. He is justifiably known and respected all over the world as a brilliant scholar, innovative theatre director and committed activist. I want to introduce Richard to you by sharing an excerpt from a recent talk of his. The topic was performance activism—this emerging global movement for social transformation through the use of play and performance—both in the form of "plays" and in how people live their day-to-day lives. Unlike the activism of the 20th century, which was for the most part ideology based and focused on politics and economics, performance activism is radically relational—a social, collaborative process of discovery and creation—of new ideas, new roles, new relationships and new activities.

In his talk at the Performing the World conference in October 2012, Richard spoke of the emergence of "a new third world" of people who relate on a performative and not an ideological basis. They are, he said, guided by the following principles:

Big Ideas and Revolutionary Activity

- To perform is to explore, to play, to experiment with new relations
- To perform is to cross borders, not only geographic but emotional, ideological, political and personal
- To perform is to engage in life-long activity study, to grasp every book as a script, as something to be played with, interpreted, reformed and remade
- To perform is to become someone else and yourself at the same time, to empathize, react, grow and change.
- These principles resonate deeply with me. What about you? Let me know and we'll perform a conversation!

A Diagnosis the DSM-5 Forgot— Physics Envy

Should psychiatrists be "heroes of uncertainty"?

Posted May 29, 2013

In his May 27, 2013 *New York Times* column, cultural and political commentator David Brooks reprimanded the compilers of the DSM-5 and contemporary psychiatry for presenting their field as scientific. At the same time, Brooks praised psychiatrists for their artistry, calling them "heroes of uncertainty" and "daring adapters, perpetually adjusting in ways more imaginative than scientific rigor."

Brooks is not the first to point out the often-vast differences between the philosophy of a social institution and the philosophy and practice of the actual people who work in a given field. (It's commonplace to read about teachers who *teach* in the face of the mandate of the institution of education to raise test scores, for example. And caring doctors who listen to their patients). But he does it well—so well, in fact, that readers might rush to make an appointment with a psychiatrist.

According to Brooks, the behavioral sciences—of which psychiatry is one—is not really a science, and so it shouldn't pretend to be one. But it does pretend—these days, with a vengeance. It's an obsession. Brooks calls it "Physics Envy."

"If the authors of the psychiatry manual want to invent a new disease, they should put Physics Envy in their handbook. The desire to be more like the hard sciences has distorted economics, education, political science, psychiatry and other behavioral fields. It's led practitioners to claim more knowledge than they can possibly have. It's devalued a certain sort of hybrid mentality that is better suited to these realms, the mentality that has one foot in the world of science and one in the liberal arts, that involves bringing multiple vantage points to human behavior."

I couldn't have said it better (although my mentor and co-author, the late philosopher and social therapist Fred Newman, and I said it many times over in our books and articles since the 1990s; see especially, *Unscientific Psychology: A Cultural-Performatory Understanding of Human Life*). To pick up on one of Brooks' important points, human behavior is uncertain. Our emotionality is incredibly complex—infinite combinations of mind, body and brain activities that act, react, mix and create with and in uniquely individual and social and cultural contexts. To misunderstand or ignore that is to *mis-treat* us.

Big Ideas and Revolutionary Activity

Brooks goes only so far, still holding fast to a disease model: "It's more important to know what sort of person has a disease than to know what sort of disease a person has." In doing so, I think he'll lose the argument every time. (Do you want an artist treating your disease?) More than that, though, he's reinforcing the belief that there's something wrong with how we're feeling and that the doctor knows how to fix it.

One of my favorite philosophers is Ludwig Wittgenstein—a brilliant, eccentric and, by his own account, tormented man. No doubt he would have been diagnosed with a mental disorder were he alive today. In his writings, he showed how trying to create *an objective science of the subjective* gives us "mental cramps," causing great confusion and pain. He said, "We can fight, hope and even believe without believing scientifically."

Another of my favorite philosophers is Fred Newman. Following Wittgenstein, he created an approach to helping people in emotional pain with a *subjective science of the subjective*. He said, "Therapy should be a culturally transforming experience, teaching us a new, and developmental, way of seeing and creating a new life."

If psychiatry heeded Wittgenstein and Newman, they might well be cured of Physics Envy.

Developmental Play for All

The creative side of culture change.

Posted April 17, 2013

Somewhere in the history of human civilization play and learning got separated. Until recently, this was unfortunate but not devastating. Now, it is, because play is rapidly being removed from our culture. Many children have no recess, physical education or free play time in school. Most well-to-do and middle class teens have lessons after school (which can turn playing at something into working at it). Most poor teens have none and no places to play. Adults work, or look for work. Play has become a luxury that, in hard times, we can't afford. The decline of play in our daily lives is happening in spite of all the research that shows play is vital to healthy human functioning.

Psychologists have long known that babies and pre-school children learn and develop through their social, imaginative and improvisational play. Adults encourage them to play and play "at"—to try new things, to stretch, to do what they do not yet "know" how to do. We praise them for playing grown up by creatively imitating what those around them do without regard to correctness. We delight in them performing as characters other than and beyond who they are. We relate to them not just as what they are capable of at the moment but simultaneously as who and what they are becoming.

For most psychologists and educators the value of play is that it facilitates the learning of social-cultural roles. Through acting out roles (play-acting), children "try out" the roles they will soon take on in "real life." I agree 100%. But I believe that there's more developmental mileage we get from playing than that. And it has to do with what Lev Vygotsky identified as the paradox of play, specifically, pretend play. Here's the paradox: when children are pretending, they are least like what they are pretending to be! When they play school they are least like teachers and students because teachers and students in school are not playing at being teachers and students, but rather acting out their societally determined roles. Children playing school, or Mommy and Daddy, or Harry Potter and Dumbledore, are not acting out predetermined roles. They're creating new performances of themselves—at once the playwrights, directors and performers. They're creating their development and learning (with our help and support, of course).

Even more, they're playing and performing and pretending pretty much full time all day long, not only when they're doing what adults call pretend play. They babble and we respond as if they're speaking our language. We relate to them as speakers when they're not (yet). We perform conversation with them. They scribble on paper or books (or walls) and we smile in delight and tell them how beautiful their picture of a tree or of Mommy is. The linking of play with theatrical performance, and then

Big Ideas and Revolutionary Activity

linking that with development is an exciting and very promising new area of research and practice. Hundreds in the US and around the globe are working to understand the developmental potential of play in this new way, as performed activity. One thing that's especially exciting about this is how the interest goes beyond early childhood in recognizing the varieties and value of developmental play throughout the life span. From organizations of play researchers and play advocates, to community organizations offering play and creative activities, to scholars, educators, youth development workers and life coaches, people are playing with play. You can find them through a Google search or contact me for some of my favorite sites, programs and people.

Become a Vygotskian!

His revolutionary ideas create a psychology of possibility and transformation.

Posted April 6, 2013

If you've ever had to read a psychology textbook, you've probably come across the name Lev Vygotsky. Most likely he was mentioned in the section of the book on child development or cognitive development and, just as likely, the book contrasted and compared him to Jean Piaget, renowned for his ideas about how children think. How unfortunate—not just for you, but for the people of the world! Because Vygotsky was so much more (Piaget was too, but that's another story).

Vygotsky lived and worked in the first decades of the Soviet Union. He did his first significant piece of work at age 19—exploring the psychology of art through Shakespeare's Hamlet—and wrote prolifically until his death from tuberculosis in 1934 at the age of 38. Despite the superficiality of the textbook Vygotsky, there's much excitement the world over for his ideas, especially on human learning and development, how important play is to development, and what speaking and thinking are. What he says is provocative and, at the same time, just plain common sense.

Vygotsky's approach was cultural. To him, human beings create who we are—on the species level and the person level—by creating culture, adapting to the culture we create, re-creating it, adapting to the re-creation, and so on.

Vygotsky's approach was social. To him, what we do we do with others—like learning to speak by having "conversations" with our mothers, brothers, sisters and fathers, long before we know the language— and that's how we become the unique person each of us is.

Vygotsky's approach was developmental. To him, what we need to be looking at is not merely who people are now, but also—and at the same time—who they are becoming. Because if we only relate to who we are and what we can do today, we'll never learn to do new things.

Vygotsky's approach was monistic and wholistic. To him, human intellect and human emotion are a unified process, not two separate and distinct human systems that compete with each other. To separate them and focus only on the intellectual, he said, creates "a one-sided view of the human personality."

I'm a Vygotskian. I find psychology without him uninspiring at best and misinformed and misinforming at worst. I think psychology tries much too hard to act like a science and gets itself into lots of trouble that way. People aren't stars or plants or organs, so trying to understand us and teach us and help us as if we were violates

Big Ideas and Revolutionary Activity

our very humanness. Vygotsky didn't do that. He tried to study human beings as the complex beings and doings that we are, not as something simpler. His is a psychology of possibility (not prediction), of development (not diagnosis), of transformation (not treatment), of hope (not hype)—and of the very human becoming activity of human be-ings.

Vygotsky's ideas have yet to be implemented on a mass scale—so entrenched are the cognitive, behavioral and individualistic biases of the psychological and educational institutions of our day. If you want to learn more and spread the word, here are a few places to start:

- *Mind in Society* (a short introduction to Vygotsky's own writing)
- *Lev Vygotsky* (a documentary film about his life and current implementations of his ideas)
- *Mind, Culture and Activity on Vimeo* (lectures and interviews with Vygotskian scholars and practitioners)
- *Lev Vygotsky: Revolutionary Scientist* (Fred Newman's and my understanding of Vygotsky's ideas and importance)
- *Vygotsky at Work and Play* (my book showing some of what the Vygotskian-izing of psychotherapy and education looks like)

Why Knowing Keeps Us Dumb

If we keep doing only what we know how to do, we'll never grow.

Posted January 4, 2014

"We live in a mass culture obsessed with the need to know at a time of such instability and unpredictability that knowing is of little good."

That is from a book I'm currently writing, entitled *The Overweight Brain: How Our Obsession with Knowing Keeps Us from Getting Smart Enough to Make a Better World*.

While the topic of human knowledge might seem esoteric, it's being discussed more widely than ever before, including its practical consequences.

Much of our lives are organized by and through the knowing paradigm, that is, through a model of understanding in which knowing precedes doing and is, indeed, considered necessary in order to do "the right thing." Amazing discoveries have been made over a few centuries, and yet it's now questionable whether this way of understanding and moving forward is any longer helping us as individuals, communities, and a species.

For years I've been speaking and teaching and practicing an alternative to the knowing paradigm that accesses our human capacity to create environments where we can explore, discover and grow. Along with philosopher and therapist Fred Newman, I wrote a book in 1997 entitled *The End of Knowing*, which put the issue this way:

> Throughout the modern era, a period of explosive growth and technological achievement, knowledge was king and understood to be the engine of human progress. But what if knowing has become an impediment to further human development? The End of Knowing addresses the practical question of how to reconstruct our world in the wake of modernism's colossal failure to solve social problems. Newman and Holzman propose "the end of knowing," in favor of "performed activity" and present the positive implications of this approach for social and educational policy.

Newman and I weren't alone in engaging the practical, world-historic issue of "how to go on." Over the last two decades there has been a lively intellectual debate over the status of knowledge and the continued viability of the knowing paradigm as the way to interact with and engage the natural and social worlds. Philosophers—especially those immersed in language, science and the foundational of mathematics—ponder how we know what we know (the area of of philosophy know as "epistemology"; they also ponder what there is to know, the area of philosophy known as "ontology."). Social scientists wonder if human life is knowable in the ways that plants and rocks and animals are. Perhaps, they suggest, we humans (and that includes the

Big Ideas and Revolutionary Activity

scientists) have varying "ways of knowing" and "a social epistemology." Even some hardcore natural scientists believe knowing may be limited and that there are some things about ourselves and the universe that we cannot ever know, no matter how hard we try. These ponderers, and others, are sometimes called postmodernists, futurists, humanists or spiritualists, and other terms I'm not so familiar with. Some directly address how therapy is done, others the field of psychology more broadly, others politics and economics. But all are worried that, from our world leaders to ordinary people, the problem isn't that we don't know yet what to do, but that we cannot solve our problems if we persist in believing that the solution lies in knowing.

Pablo Picasso and Albert Einstein are quoted so often, I was hesitant at first to repeat their famous sayings. But I decide to, because, for me, they speak directly to the human predicament the knowing paradigm has gotten us into. Two quotes will do to show the muddle we're in. Commenting on his trade, the great artist Picasso said, "Every child is an artist. The problem is how to remain an artist once we grow up." And the brilliant theoretical physicist Einstein advised, "We cannot solve our problems with the same thinking we used when we created them."

Both Picasso and Einstein are pointing to the same trap we're in—once we know how to do something, we become less willing and able to do new things. We get stuck doing what we know how to do. Imagination reigns supreme when we're little—when we don't yet know that we're supposed to know. We take risks. We learn how to paint, draw, sing, dance, talk, even think, because we "paint" "draw" "sing" "dance" "talk" and even "think" without knowing how! Before we know, we do. We play, we perform, we pretend our way to growth, learning and knowledge. This is the fundamental developmental process of the human species.

To remain an artist as an adult, then, we can't let all the knowledge we've accumulated about art, color, perspective, how things are supposed to look, etc. take over, or suppress our imagination and stop us from doing things with paint and pencil that we've never done before. And it's the same with thinking. By the time we're adults, most of us know how to think, and for a big portion of our lives, that way works pretty well. But not always. And when it doesn't, we need to let go of "I know what to do" and generate new ways of thinking about the situation. "I know" only keeps us dumb.

The way out of this predicament, as far as I can tell, is to grow beyond knowing. By that I mean to create environments in which people of all ages can do things without knowing how. These are environments for creativity, play, performance and becoming. These are the types of environments that we create for and with babies and toddlers. These are environments that have at their root a new conception of human development as becoming who we are by performing who we are not. Einstein and Picasso seem to not only have raised the questions that "performing who we are not" answers; it seems that their lives and works embody it.

Meet the Editors

Now that we have introduced you to Lois, we wanted to share a little more about who we are. Some of this might be ego. When you edit a book, you don't want to completely disappear from its pages! But there is another reason. We chose to edit this book together because of the impact that Lois has had on our lives and on the work that we are doing now and will do in the future. We hope that by sharing our stories and the ways Lois has helped us become the activist scholars we are today, we will continue to inspire you to see how the chapters in this book are part of an ongoing, living, breathing activity that you are now a part of.

Carrie

Lois' work has inspired and sustained me for over two decades. The paths she blazed gave me the chutzpah (nerve) to write a dissertation on early childhood education that challenged traditional understandings of child development. It provided me with the references I needed to publish articles on improv comedy in prestigious academic journals, and it has given me a way to break out of the limited silos of the university to become an activist scholar who works with educators, psychologists, doctors, community organizers, actors, architects and more.

I grew up in a family with a radical politic and a traditional psychology. My parents were Marxists and revolutionaries--and they were actively engaged in the process of making a revolution. For my parents, and particularly my mother, this radical politic lived side by side with a fairly traditional and I would say conservative set of beliefs about psychology and psychotherapy. I grew up seeing psychology as separate from politics--and that the merging of the two was unethical and dangerous.

I started college in 1982. When I decided to major in psychology I saw nothing political about the choice; actually, if anything, I saw it as a move away from politics. I became a psychology major, as many people do, because I hoped to understand others and myself better by studying how human beings work. I didn't see psychology as having a politic or even as coming out of a particular time or context.

After graduation I became a preschool teacher, and it gradually became clear to me that traditional approaches to psychology, far from being apolitical, were inseparable from the social structure of the world and that they served to perpetuate and support the status quo. I began teaching preschool in 1986 at a private nursery school in Greenwich Village in New York City. The children in my class came from primarily upper middle class and wealthy professional families. Steeped in a child-centered philosophy that had evolved over the previous fifty years to be loosely based on Erikson's psychosocial stages of development, Piagetian stages of cognitive development and a Deweyan belief in active experiences with real-life materials, these psychological theories helped justify a curriculum that taught children that they were the center of the universe and that how *they felt* was the most important thing in the world. It also placed me, the teacher, in the position of being an experience provider, or as

Big Ideas and Revolutionary Activity

I came to see it, a waitress. I had the experience that, while the children were active all day long, they were learning to expect the world to revolve around them. I had spent time in poor and working class childcare centers as a student and I knew this was not the universal curriculum. And more than that, my struggles with the parents of these children confirmed that the "me" focused curriculum had lifelong effects.

The preschool provided a few scholarships to children of color from poor communities. The school had a liberal politic; no one would ever say that the culture of these children, or their communities, was "deprived," but every single one of these children ended up being diagnosed with a psychological problem. Every. Single. One. And this was justified, not by a critique of their culture, but by comparing them to the psychological norms of the stage theories that were in vogue. This experience, viewed through the lens of my political upbringing, made me, to say the least, uneasy.

Soon after college, I met Lois and the community she was a part of and was introduced to an approach to therapy, education, and human development called Social Therapeutics. I discovered a group of people who were overtly and unabashedly political in their therapeutic and educational work and who spoke openly about the politics of how children were taught. I know that I had incredible luck meeting Lois so early in my career. I was a political person, doing what I then considered an apolitical job. Through my work with Lois, I have been able to create a life where there is no separation between my desire to make the world a better place and my life as an academic.

Tony

I am (becoming) a teacher/improviser/community builder/developmentalist/academic. While these descriptions feel appropriate at this time and place in history, they have at once built upon each other and occurred simultaneously. I began teaching adults from around the world English as a new language in 1991, and it is with/in the activity of teaching adults that I discovered and first co-created possibilities for play and performance. As an undergraduate student, I was released from traditional university expectations such as distribution requirements and specialization in a particular area of study. As such, I was able to design my own program of study; the only requirement was a culminating project that integrated my program of study. I focused my program of study on creative writing, literature, acting, linguistics and languages. I particularly enjoyed my acting classes and the holism of the learning/development of these classes. The activities in these classes developed sensory/body awareness, group dynamics, vocal practice and reflective capacities.

I felt the varied and engaging activities in these acting classes might also have some relevance to the teaching I had been doing with adults learning English. Activities from/inspired by these acting classes were a welcomed antidote to the toxicity of overly transmissive and heavily behaviorist approaches to (language) learning I had had as a student and teacher. My experiences with/in acting classes re-established the importance of being playful with others. Based on these experiences and insights, my culminating project was the design, teaching, and reflection/analysis of a fourteen-week course that was based on activities of drama, improv, mime and other creative endeavors offered to a group of international adults in the community who were intermediate to advanced users of English as a new language. This course proved to be a powerful and new learning, teaching and community building possibility for my students and me. Over the course of more than 20 years, I taught, learned from and built community with adult language learners from many countries of origin, of a range of ages, with unique experiences with formal schooling, with diverse intentions to learn, and in a host of different formal and informal learning contexts—and drew upon/co-created playful and performatory activities to do so.

In 2001, I moved from the suburbs of New York City to Chicago, Illinois, to study and perform improvisational theater (improv). While studying and performing improv in Chicago, I not only continued teaching adults English as a new language, but I was also employed in programs working with youth and communities of color and as an academic professional at the University of Illinois at Chicago (UIC). I began my graduate studies in education at UIC in 2003, focusing on human development and learning with/in/via play and performance.

It was not until 2004, as a new master's student at UIC, that I met Lois and her work. In fact, I first connected to Lois and her work via Carrie, after having searched online for others in academia who taught/researched the possibilities of improv to promote learning and teaching. Carrie introduced me to Lois, and Lois shared her work with me. Lois's work instantly revolutionized my understandings of play, performance and the possibilities and power of collaborative, emergent group activity to effect revolutionary development and learning. While Lois' work may have come a good number of years after I had begun "playing with play," my teaching/scholarship/community building would from then on be primarily informed and inspired by my interactions with Lois and her work. I have not only continuously engaged (with)/performed Lois' work, but I have also had the privilege and joy to perform with Lois at academic conferences, international gatherings of Performing the World, and in online courses/activities on social therapeutics.

I graduated from UIC in 2013 and was a faculty member at the University of Memphis for a year. I have been a faculty member at the University of Washington Tacoma (UWT) since 2014, where I teach courses in human development and lifespan imaginative play. I draw upon my varied experiences as an improviser and academic to teach, learn and build community in my classes/at UWT and around the world via play and performance. I am infinitely grateful to Lois and her community building/scholarship/activism that has inspired and developed a transformational, holistic journey of teaching/community work/scholarship/activism via play, performance and improvisation.